LESSONS FROM
HISTORY

Project Lessons
from the
Roman Empire

An Ancient Guide to
Modern Project Management

"There is nothing new in this world except the history you do not know."

- Harry S. Truman

Project Lessons from the Roman Empire

An Ancient Guide to Modern Project Management

Author
Jerry Manas

First Edition

Multi-Media Publications Inc.

Oshawa, Ontario

Project Lessons from the Roman Empire: An Ancient Guide to Modern Project Management
By Jerry Manas

Editor:	Kevin Aguanno
Typesetting:	Tak Keung Sin
Cover Design:	Cheung Hoi
eBook Conversion:	Agustina Baid

Published by:
Multi-Media Publications Inc.
Box 58043, Rosslynn RPO, Oshawa, Ontario, Canada, L1J 8L6.

http://www.mmpubs.com/

ISBN-13 (Paperback):	9781554890545
ISBN-13 (Adobe PDF eBook):	9781554890552

Published in Canada. Printed simultaneously in the U.S.A. and Great Britain.

CIP data available from the publisher.

Table of Contents

Acknowledgments

There are so many people that have always been there for inspiration and support that to thank all of them would require a book in itself. I must of course thank my agent, Daniel Bial, not only for the years of support and representation, but also for the keen advice on all of my manuscripts over the years. Daniel, your comments are always right on the money. I must also thank Kevin Aguanno of Multi-Media Publications. Kevin has been trying to get me to do this book for years and I'm glad we were finally able to make it happen. Kevin's stellar editors and designers made my life easy with their formatting, design, photographs, and illustrations. Thanks also to fellow author and history aficionado Mark Kozak-Holland, who put me in touch with Kevin and encouraged me to do this book. Mark and I should do a "lessons from history" road show (note to self).

I of course must thank my wife Sharon for once again supporting my writing efforts, and my daughter Elizabeth for inspiring nearly everything I do in life. She's the reason I do all this, so that one day when she grows up and enters the working world, maybe by chance her managers will have read my books and she won't have to work for morons. Better yet, maybe she'll own her own company and use the books to lead others responsibly.

Thanks to Dave Garrett, CEO of Gantthead.com, for giving me a fun place to write my sometimes off-the-wall articles, and for allowing me to leverage much of my Rome article series (which originally appeared on Gantthead) in the making of this book. Thanks also to my fellow co-founders of the Project Management Institute's *New Media Council:* Len O'Neal, Dave Garrett (again), Cornelius Fichtner, Hal Macomber, Elizabeth Harrin, Chalyce Nollsch, Josh Nankival, Raven Young, and Bas De Bar. I learn from you guys every day.

I cannot forget to thank my parents, Sid and Barbara, and my brother Eric, for their endless support, as well as Dr. Norman Olson and Sallie Olson. I wrote about the importance of family, and I am truly grateful to have such wonderful family in my life.

Special thanks to my friends and colleagues at The Creating WE Institute. I cannot just name a few as all of them are like family. I must at least mention Judith Glaser, who's been a true friend and a huge inspiration. Judith has been doing groundbreaking research on neuroscience as it applies to leadership. Through her work, organizations are learning how to have truly transformational conversations in the workplace. Last, but not least, thanks to my PMThink! colleagues, Frank Miller, Graham McHardy, and Garry Booker.

Introduction

I t's been said that all roads lead to Rome. If we look at lessons in leadership and project management, this is certainly true. Consider just a few examples of the amazing legacy the Roman Empire has left us:

- **Roads**: The Romans were the absolute masters of building roads, an activity that served many purposes. When they first started their conquering, Europe and the Near East were a patchwork of villages and small fiefdoms. By putting in roads, Rome gathered together and shrank the known world. Roads allowed their armies to move faster, to conquer more, and to keep control of the conquered lands. It vastly improved trade. It allowed them to export their culture, as well as import the best that belonged to the cultures of those conquered. And Roman roads have withstood the test of time. One can still travel roads initially built 2,000 years ago. The Appian Way is merely one example.

- **Aqueducts**: The Romans were masters of bringing water from one place to another. The aqueducts were marvels of engineering, and they too still stand, 2000 years later.

- **Warfare**: Roman soldiers were better trained and equipped than all their enemies. Their speed—on the roads they built—overwhelmed many a foe.

- **Laws**: Rome created the first real legal system, a tremendous breakthrough in the growth of civilization.

- **Public buildings and art**: We still marvel at the Colisseum, and many amphitheatres around the world. Roman painting and sculpture was also renowned.

- **Plumbing**: Romans not only created indoor plumbing for the houses of the wealthy, they also created the greatest sewer system of the time (Rome's Cloaca Maxima), and were able to drain marshes and build elaborate baths—all major breakthroughs in terms of health.

- **Castles and forts**: Romans built strong defensive buildings all over the world. One can still see the impressive buildings Rome left behind from Britain to Israel, across Europe and northern Africa.

- **Fire laws**: Nero supposedly fiddled while Rome burned. But Rome was a firetrap at the time, with wood buildings piled higgledy-piggledy. After the great fire, they blazed the way to institute fire safety precautions.

- **Bread and circuses**: The Romans knew to keep the people fed, amused and happy, which went a long way to encourage "buy in" and reduce riots.

- **Leadership**: The Romans had some incredible leaders who made lasting impacts in different ways, Augustus being one example. Of course, certain emperors, such as Nero and Caligula, exemplified the rule about absolute power tending to corrupt absolutely. On the other hand, the Romans tended to not let such monsters go on too long.

- **Succession Planning**: The Romans had a way of allowing the caesarship to pass along in family lines even when blood relatives weren't up to the job. They "adopted" their favorites, even when the one they were tapping to be next in line was already a fully mature adult. Emperors-in-waiting took the name of Caesar, and when they became emperor they'd take the name Augustus.

Any society that can achieve such a continued level of innovation, growth, and advancement is worthy of studying. It is through lessons from the past that we can learn to make good decisions in the future. We can be better equipped to lead people, more purposeful in our planning, and more inspired to innovate. We can also avoid the mistakes of the past, being more aware of the implications of our actions. As Mark Twain said, "History doesn't repeat itself, but it does rhyme."[*]

---

[*] *I first heard this quote at a seminar given by Edward Tufte, the noted guru on information presentation. He also cited T.S. Eliot's great statement that "Talent imitates, genius steals." So I stole the Twain quote from Tufte.*

Lessons, Lessons, Everywhere

When doing research, I often search for lessons that are applicable to both leadership and project management. Indeed, the two are indelibly intertwined. It is the goal of any leader to effectively achieve objectives through people. To do this requires knowledge of the vision and inspiration that great leadership brings and the planning, tracking, and communication methods of sound project management.

The Roman Empire had great leaders and poor leaders, and we'll learn from all of them. Their empire lasted centuries, with unsurpassed accomplishments in project management, including warfare projects, construction projects, civil development projects, all serving one overall purpose—the preservation, expansion, and advancement of the Roman way of life. To this end, the Roman Empire could be considered a corporaion, with a collection of *programs and project portfolios* supporting the overall mission. In a sense, this was "early program and portfolio management" being conducted by the equivalent of a mega-corporation, such as GE or IBM.

And yet the great empire fell. This too, brings us lessons, as there were plenty of warning signs.

As they say, "Rome wasn't built in a day," so we have much to cover. With this in mind, we will take an organized approach, first exploring the underlying principles and skills that enabled Rome to become what it was in the first place—then examining their methods in detail and their way of life. Having built this foundation, we will look at Roman history from a bird's-eye view: first examining the rise of Rome, from monarchy to republic to empire; and then examining the decline and fall of the seemingly invincible Roman Empire. Along the way we will extract lessons—lessons in leadership, strategy, project management, and cultural awareness—lessons that we can immediately apply today.

How do we know so much about ancient Rome? Fortunately, there is more known about the Romans than virtually any other ancient civilization, mainly because they were a highly educated society and documented everything. Most famously, Julius Caesar authored several books detailing his military campaigns and strategy, and Suetonius offered first and second hand accounts in his book, *The Twelve Caesars*. Many artifacts have been discovered as well that have shed light on their construction and engineering techniques. Many of their creations are not only still standing today, but are in regular use, giving us first-hand experiences with Roman technology.

Unfortunately, there is no single searchable database of "lessons learned" from ancient Rome, so I gathered lessons the old-fashioned way, researching a variety of sources including books and scholarly websites. Of course, having to mine for information is fine (and expected) when researching ancient history, but you wouldn't want to have to dig through multiple sources in order to extract lessons from recently completed projects. We are at least fortunate that the Romans documented so much, not only in their writings, but through stone inscriptions detailing laws, legal contracts, financial transactions and military records. Therefore, before we even begin, our first lesson is:

Be sure to document lessons learned throughout your project, while things are fresh in your mind. At the end of your project, finalize them in a useful summary format geared toward its intended target audience, not buried in issues lists and change logs. Better yet, keep a database updated with lessons learned by category.

Foundations of Success: Why did Rome Rise?

Before attempting to extract lessons from the rise of the Roman Empire, it is important to understand the underlying Roman principles that fostered its growth, namely: belief in the gods (they believed the gods wanted them to proliferate their civilized way of life throughout the world); necessity of learning from the past (no, that's not just a shameless plug); strength of the family; education through books and public service; and last, but not least, obedience. Obedience was important to ensure proper execution of project directives. We'll talk more about other ways to accomplish this later, as the mere word *obedience* isn't likely to win over any employees or serve as motivation. What we're really looking for is *alignment*.

The central philosophy of ancient Rome was *Stoicism*, originally founded by the Hellenistic Greeks. Stoicism declares that logic and self-control can overcome all. And self-control was needed because for the Stoic the meaning of each individual life, action, and situation was determined by its place in a larger, predestined whole. The Stoics felt that life had to be harmonious with the universe, over which one has no control. But, as mentioned, the Romans believed that their universal calling was that the gods wanted them to expand their rule of law (called "The Law of Nations"), so this was very convenient indeed—an undeniable mission.

In addition to a convincing "reason for being," there were several other elements that aided the spread of the Roman Empire. First, they used a franchise approach. What they offered to potential franchisees (i.e. neighboring cities) were the rights and privileges of Roman citizenship, or at least good government, security, and a reasonable justice system. People preferred to be ruled by Rome, for the alternatives were either uncivilized barbarians to the north or tyranny to the east and south. Also, some kings without heirs left their kingdoms to the Romans, seeing Rome as the best governor of their people after their own death.

"That's fine," you say, "but what does all this have to do with project management?" Well, there are two primary lessons here: one being the importance of aligning your project with the company's strategic plan (which as mentioned, like God's plan, is typically beyond your control), and the other being to sell your people on the project by positioning your project to be better than any alternative (which, luckily, you do have some control over). The same applies to selling the concept of a Project Management Office, or PMO.

Let's look at each lesson in more detail.

Strategy and Alignment

Before you attempt to align your project with the company's strategic goal, you must first address an inherent problem. That is, as a project manager, not only are you typically not in control of the company's strategic plan; you're typically not even in control of your project's charter, which contains the business need and the description of the product that the project is supposed to deliver.

The charter usually comes from management external to the project, and is hopefully already aligned with a corporate objective (which, in an ideal world, was how the project got approved in the first place). The project manager, in turn, takes it from there, ensuring that the objectives on the charter are met through proper planning and implementation.

So, if it turns out that the charter was *not* aligned with a corporate objective to begin with, how does a project manager go about ensuring that their project is aligned with a corporate objective? And the even bigger question: why bother? If the sponsor or customer didn't care when the charter was created, why should the project manager care now?

Let's begin by addressing the question of "how." If your company does not have a formal portfolio management process (meant to tie projects to strategic corporate goals), the best method is to simply ask the requester, either verbally (or better yet) via a formal project request form, what is the corporate or department objective with which this project is aligned. This may take some pressing or creative framing if it is not immediately apparent. Be sure to document this with the project records, in the charter and/or other documentation.

17

This alignment is important because it is the project's justification for existence—its call to action. This takes us to the "why bother" question. Why do we care about the project's justification if the initial charter has already been approved? There are several reasons.

First, it aids in selling the project team on the project and getting them motivated. Feeling that they're part of something important motivates project team members, just as it does troops in the military. It is the project manager's job to make the project seem important to the team (hopefully it won't be too much of a stretch because people can tell the difference). The good news is that just about anything can be made to feel important, especially if it's tied to an overall corporate or departmental goal.

Tom Peters stresses this in his book, *The Professional Service Firm 50* (and has often repeated the theme in his books and presentations on passion and innovation in the workplace). Peters states that each department in an organization should operate like a Professional Services Firm (whose members he refers to as PSFers), and should frame all work to be client-centric project work. Specifically, he says:

> "100 percent of your time should be occupied by discrete projects. This is not pie-in-the-sky. The most mundane tasks-in the hands of a thoughtful PSFer – can be converted into interesting probes into the heart of a business system; that is, Projects Worth Doing (E.g.; A McKinsey & Co. colleague, Bill Matassoni, converted a 'dreary' library reorg chore into a strategic knowledge-sharing initiative that changed the entire company.)

> My uncompromising, unequivocal point here:
> One hundred percent – no rounding error! – of
> 'Dept.' work CAN be converted to Client-centric
> Project Work.
>> 'We' (PSFers) live for our ...Clients. We live to
>> do ...Projects. That's it. That's all. And if you can't
>> convert 'it' (the 'mundane' task) to a Client-centric
>> Project? Well... drop it. Cold. Now."

Radical? Maybe. But it certainly generates passion and dedication, which is all too often lacking in the workplace. Plus it can elevate results considerably.

The second reason we should care about the project's justification is that it provides the basis for evaluating tradeoffs, should stakeholders request changes to the project or should tradeoffs in time, scope, or cost be needed. In other words, it provides focus. Which tradeoffs are agreed upon will depend largely on the ultimate objective the project is meant to fulfill.

So the lesson here is:

Make sure to document the business need, tied to a corporate or departmental objective, as part of your project's charter and/or scope statement. This is useful for keeping the team motivated by making the project important, and for providing much needed focus, especially when evaluating future tradeoffs.

"This is all very fine," you say, "but what does it have to do with ancient Rome?" It becomes clear when we see that the Romans aligned all of their projects with the ultimate goal of expanding their empire. The business need was to proliferate their "Law of Nations" throughout the world to fulfill their god-given mandate. Any changes to their plan would be weighed against whether it served the ultimate goal and the business need. Above all, it served to keep people dedicated to the mission, especially when weighed against the alternatives. This is what marketing people refer to as "positioning." The Romans used positioning extremely well, and this leads us to our next lesson from the rise of the Roman Empire.

Purpose and Positioning

The word "positioning" is somewhat of a misnomer. Marketing people use the term to refer to the process of creating your position in the public's mind as compared to other choices. It implies that you can create your position but in reality you cannot. The public gives you your real position. You can only create the image of your desired position and possibly influence the public—not by lying, mind you, but by choosing the opposition that you will compare yourself to. Call it creative framing.

Rome used positioning by convincing the public that their ways were better than any alternative—be it "uncivilized" barbarians or dictatorship (never mind that Rome had its share of dictators throughout its history). They knew that people often are motivated by fear of the alternative or some other strong emotion. As Cicero said, "Men decide far more problems by hate, love, lust, rage, sorrow, joy, hope, fear, illusion, or some other inward emotion, than by reality, authority, any legal standard, judicial precedent, or statute."

Project managers can potentially use the same tactic to motivate their team by comparing the project to the (hopefully) less desirable alternative of not doing the project, or any other alternative, for that matter. The best source of this analysis is the project justification and overall corporate objective it's meant to satisfy.

That's not to say that positioning is the only way to motivate your team, just that it's one of the ways that is often overlooked. It's good for getting team buy-in, which is important for a successful project, especially a large-scale one. In my book *Napoleon on Project Management*, I noted that one of the several causes of the failed Russian Campaign of 1812 was that many of Napoleon's troops deserted before they even got to Russia. This is because the deserters were mostly foreign troops from conquered lands, and therefore not as dedicated to the mission. Indeed, the same thing happened to Rome, as we will see later. Undedicated team members can cause havoc on a project. Gaining buy-in by making sure the project's need is perceived and by positioning your project to be better than any alternatives (from your audience's perspective) can go along way to prevent that.

Of course, one thing that greatly assists in influencing the position of your project in your audience's mind is *focus*. We've already talked about how having a clear business need tied to a corporate goal adds focus. Another trick to provide focus is one that is often used by marketers, and that is to say one thing, and one thing only. Harry Beckwith discusses this in his classic book on service marketing, *Selling the Invisible – A Field Guide to Modern Marketing*. In his book, Beckwith states that people create anchors (or associations) in their mind, and will rarely remember a complicated or multi-tiered message. This may mean sacrificing some information, but much can be gained by associating your project with one major goal or battle cry when selling the project to your team (although all related business initiatives should still be listed in the project documentation).

In other words, reinforcing your project's "reason for being" with a singularly focused message helps solidify your position; however, it is not enough. You must also "create" the position of your competitor in your audience's mind (in this case, the competitor being an alternative solution—typically not doing the project). Without anything to compare it to, your project has no position.

The good news is that the cost of not doing the project should already included in the business case, and is usually analyzed when weighing alternatives during scope planning. Thus, it should be readily available. If it is not, you'll need to do some research. The bottom line is that you want your project's position to be obviously better than any alternative, especially the alternative of not doing the project. This makes it clear to your project team—and to stakeholders—that the project is worthwhile.

Often, properly framing a project requires some business acumen—that is, you must understand the basic building blocks of any business and use that knowledge to figure out how your company makes money and operates as a business. Ram Charan, in his book, *What the CEO Wants You to Know*, states that a good manager must have both leadership skills and business acumen, and must cut through the complexity within and outside of the organization to understand the big picture. Of course, the best place to start developing business acumen is to read Charan's book, so I will not go into the details here (and risk straying too far from our focus on ancient Rome). Charan's book is a quick read and, as the title says, explains what the CEO of any company would love everyone in the organization to know—namely, the fundamentals of any organization.

One last book I'll suggest is *Made to Stick* by Chip and Dan Heath. This fascinating book explores why some messages or ideas stick and others do not. The authors use the SUCCESs acronym to define the key components of a "sticky" message:

- **Simple** (Say one central thing in plain language)
- **Unexpected** (Don't dump facts; Pique interest instead)
- **Concrete** (Use examples, analogies, nouns; Avoid abstract concepts)
- **Credible** (Offer details, simple statistics, and credible reference points)
- **Emotional** (Play to a fear or need; human interest—emphasize benefits as opposed to features)
- **Story** (An example or case study; Simulating past events is more powerful than envisioning future outcomes)

Anyone looking to sell any idea or concept would be wise to follow this advice. Meanwhile, before we return to ancient Rome, let's remember this lesson:

To reinforce the importance of your project, give your project a reason for being, and position your project in your team's mind to be better than any alternative (including not doing the project). Make a compelling case by applying business acumen. The Romans made effective use of positioning by offering security and stability as opposed to tyranny or barbarism.

CHAPTER TWO

Ensuring a Disciplined Team

One of the most important principles of the Roman Empire was obedience. They could have the best plans, the most motivated troops, but if they couldn't be sure their plans would be followed to the letter, that their soldiers would be more disciplined than the enemy, they could not be assured of success.

To ensure obedience, the Romans sometimes used brutal methods of persuasion. Occasionally, if someone in the military were caught disobeying orders, one out of ten people in their legion would be executed, and not necessarily the one breaching the order (this is where the modern term "to decimate" came from). This not only discouraged offenders, but also created a self-policing system, as nobody wanted to die

Figure 2.1 - The roman flagellum was a whip with weighted ends used for corporal punishment of soldiers.

because of someone else's offense. But this harshness wasn't necessarily the rule. Often a simple clarification was adequate.

For example, Julius Caesar, in his book, *The Conquest of Gaul*, lectured a soldier for attempting a risky maneuver, as depicted in the following excerpt from his book (translated by S.A. Handford and revised by Jane F. Gardner). Note that Caesar always referred to himself in the third person, at least when writing.

> "The next day Caesar paraded the troops and reprimanded them for their rashness and impetuosity. They had decided for themselves, he said, to advance farther and attack the town, neither halting when the retreat was sounded nor obeying the military tribunes and generals who tried to restrain them. He stressed the disadvantage of an unfavorable position, explaining the motives which had dictated his action at Avaricum, when, although he had caught the enemy without their general or their cavalry, he preferred to sacrifice a certain victory rather than to incur even light casualties by fighting on unfavorable ground.
>
> 'Much as I admire the heroism that you showed,' he went on, 'in refusing to be daunted by a fortified camp, a high mountain, and a walled fortress, I cannot too strongly condemn your bad

discipline and your presumption in thinking that you
knew better than your commander-in-chief how to
win a victory or to foresee the results of an action. I
want obedience and self-restraint from my soldiers,
just as much as courage in the face of danger.'
He concluded his speech with words of encouragement, telling the men not to be upset by a
reverse, which was due to their unfavorable position
and not to the enemy's fighting quality."

There's much to be learned from this little speech. First,
Caesar favored "planned audacity"—that is, he knew the importance of speed and capitalizing on an opportunity, but not
at the expense of planning, and certainly not with undue risk
to project outcomes. Second, and more aligned with our topic,
he valued obedience over reckless heroism. Third, he brought
to light the fact that people in the heat of action are generally
not fully aware of the strategic perspective and context.

That is not to say that creativity and inspiration should not
be encouraged, nor that the team is not as smart as the project
manager, merely that people should not go off and do their
own thing, especially if it involves altering the agreed-upon
scope and deliverables. The project manager is most fully aware
of the performance statistics, risks, and broad stakeholder implications, and therefore needs to orchestrate project outcomes
accordingly. To the extent that people are engaged in these
items, the project manager can afford some leeway.

There is a fine line between controlling a project's strategy
and outcomes versus micromanaging the actions that lead to
the outcomes. We want people to be creative and innovative.
We want them to be engaged and motivated. We also want to

be cognizant of the fact that they are often the experts in their function. We do *not* want them to independently change the strategic approach or alter the agreed-upon scope or objectives, though they should be encouraged to provide input and make suggestions. Today's project manager needs to ensure that the team is aligned with the plan, and we have proven methods today that are effective at accomplishing this without requiring blind adherence to an overly detailed plan. Let's explore some of these methods.

Control without Micromanagement – Modern Methods for Assuring Alignment

The old hierarchical management style is no longer considered effective or desirable in the business world, and even the military is now exploring more participatory leadership methods. Today's project manager must be a leader, a facilitator, and a coach, not just a manager or administrator. He or she must know how to solicit ideas and feedback and engage people in the planning process. Nowhere is this more important than in the execution phase of a project. However, all too often, this becomes the "forgotten phase" with most of the time being dedicated to planning and closeout (using the filmmaker's approach of "always leave 'em with a good ending"), and virtually none spent on communicating, monitoring, and reporting during project execution.

This line of thinking seems to assume that, since the project was so well planned, we can now rest until it's over and then spend our efforts tidying up loose ends and advertising the huge success during closeout reporting. The problem is that there are countless things that can go wrong when a project isn't monitored closely, and the project manager must then scurry to perform damage control.

So, how does one ensure an aligned team without micromanaging or using an overly hierarchical leadership style? One way is to be sure everyone understands the project's goals. Albert Einstein said, "Confusion of goals and perfections of means seems, in my opinion, to characterize our age." This statement holds true in project management as well. We need to be sure everyone, including the team and stakeholders, is aligned on the goals of the project.

In addition, we need to focus on controlling expected outcomes and deliverables by assigning *work packages* to individuals or sub-teams. A work package defines a deliverable or section of the project, provides objectives and guidelines for achieving the objectives, and authorizes someone to own and manage that work package in line with the outcomes and guidelines. This ensures alignment but leaves the accountability for the execution of activities in the hands of the experts who are performing them. It also encourages distributed leadership. In conjunction with the work package approach, a brief milestones list also helps to track progress toward key milestones.

We also need to boost team communication, perhaps through daily check-ins, or even through social media tools such as Twitter or Yammer (which is like Twitter except it can be secured, making it more appealing for corporate use). Successfully run, a brief, frequent check-in is not micromanagement. On the contrary, it serves to avoid micromanagement because it adequately keeps the project manager and the team in touch with the project status and important related issues.

When Augustus rose to power in 27 BC, ending years of civil war and issuing reforms that led to 150 years of peace in Ancient Rome, the poet Horace likened him to a helmsman who had steered a ship into safe port. Just like Augustus, the project manager must steer the project into safe port. It's much easier to keep a ship on course when making frequent adjustments due to ever changing wind conditions. And it's easier to make these adjustments when there are regular check-ins.

One way to do this is through periodic check-in meetings. These check-in meetings don't have to be long (in fact they should be brief and exception-oriented), nor do they necessarily have to be in person (it can be a teleconference); they just need to cover the following:

- The overall objective and business need (you can't repeat this often enough)

- The overall project status and stakeholder satisfaction level

- What major milestones have been completed since the last meeting, if any?

- What major milestones are coming up in the next period, if any?

- What open or new issues are there that need to be discussed in this time period? If the project is off track, what is needed to bring it back on track?

- What risks have emerged since the last meeting? Do we need to make changes to the project plan or execute any risk contingencies as a result?

- Have there been any new lessons that would be worthy of adding to the list of "lessons learned?"

Documenting lessons learned is something that should be added to each team meeting as part of an ongoing process. It is during the project that these things are thought of, not at the end of the project when people typically try to do this. By that time, many crucial things would likely have been forgotten.

Likewise, risk management is something that should be an ongoing process and covered at each meeting, not as a one-time effort at the beginning of the project. It also serves to get the team involved in the process of thinking about risk, which further reduces the need for micromanagement.

Finally, stakeholder satisfaction should be gauged throughout the project and not just at the end when it's too late to do anything about it. Getting frequent feedback not only keeps stakeholders engaged and lets them know you care, it allows for early correction of issues and assures no surprises at the end.

In addition to clear goals, defined work packages, and frequent check-ins, it is critical for the project manager to practice the art of MBWA (management by wandering around). Again, the purpose of this is not to micromanage, which is unnecessary and is typically a de-motivator. It's to get a sense of what is happening on a daily basis and to make yourself available to your team should they have informal questions. Even in casual conversation, things come up that can make or break a project. So it's well worthwhile making a point to leave the office or cubicle sometimes. Even General George S. Patton recognized this when he said, in typical Patton style, "I've never judged an officer by the calluses on his butt."

Needless to say, there is plenty for the project manager to do to keep a project under control, making the execution phase every bit as critical as the planning phase.

To summarize, let's remember this lesson regarding obedience:

> Don't forget the Project Execution phase. What the Romans called "Obedience" and we can call "Alignment" can be achieved by having clear and agreed-upon goals; assigned work packages; brief, frequent check-ins that include issues, risks, lessons learned, and stakeholder feedback; and good old MBWA (management by wandering around). This will allow you to steer the ship into safe port (as Horace noted that Augustus had done).

CHAPTER THREE

Work/Life Integration: Building Community

Cornelia was a Roman matron in the 2nd century BC, noted for her virtue and intelligence. One day, a woman from Campania boasted of her jewels. In response, Cornelia pointed to her sons and replied, "There are *my* jewels." Cornelia was well known for instilling courage, intellect, and civic duty in her sons, who were unfortunately killed while attempting to enact land reforms. A statue was erected in her honor when she died. In Rome, family and education meant everything. They recognized this as a core part of any civilized society and knew that it would be the backbone of their future. Certainly they weren't the first to recognize this, nor were they the last.

Stephen Covey touched on the importance of both family and education in his landmark book, *The 7 Habits of Highly Effective People*. The third habit, "Put First Things First" stresses the importance of focusing priorities, and being sure to make room for the important, but not urgent things. This includes balancing all of the key roles in your life, including family, work, and public service. The seventh habit, "Sharpen the Saw," refers to the importance of maintaining the physical, spiritual, intellectual and emotional self. This can be accomplished in numerous ways, including, but not limited to, exercise, reading and attending classes.

As Covey stresses, and as the Romans knew, to be truly effective in life, we must never forget the importance of family and community. Also we must consistently strive to seek self-renewal and self-improvement through reading, exercise, public service, and education. For more on this and the remaining five habits, I highly recommend reading Covey's classic book.

The Romans were social creatures, which is why they favored the city. There, they could be around family, friends, and social events—and could belong to a community. An extended family, whether rich or poor, would all live under one roof. Men would work an early six-hour day (as advanced as the Romans were, women still did not work in these days) and would spent much of the afternoon in the public baths socializing before returning home for dinner and family time. To the Romans, the city offered a chance to evolve from merely being peasants living off of the land to being members of society. To them, this was "civilization," and the countryside was reserved for the occasional nature outing.

The city also offered the Forum, a bustling public space filled with open squares, businesses, kiosks, courtrooms, and meeting halls. It was closed to vehicles during the day to create a vibrant pedestrian area. The Forum was a place where people mingled and where many deals were made. Each emperor added increasingly glorious architecture, making the Forum a place to behold. Surrounding the Forum were streets lined with shops and markets.

Figure 3.1 - The entrance to the Roman Forum as it stands today.

There was also a complex, underlying social structure made up of various social classes based on heredity, property and wealth, as well as a "client system" that played a role in one's rise through the hierarchy. As stated in the PBS website on Ancient Rome (http://www.pbs.org/empires/romans/):

> "Roman society was also defined by an established system of patronage, in which an upper class gentleman — patroni — offered protection to freedmen, or members of the lower class — cliens. That protection might take the form of financial assistance, the provision of food, or legal help. Traditionally, any freed slaves became the cliens of their former owner.
>
> In return, the patroni received respect and political favors. During the Empire cliens were required to offer daily greetings to their patroni, and the number of these salutatores, or greeters, were noted in determining someone's social status."[*]

This loyalty (which the Romans referred to as *Fides*) was one of the very foundations of Roman society, and extended not only to the patron and client, but to their families as well, remaining intact for generations.

As we can see, although their social structure had many faults (privileges of heredity and class being a case in point), family and business were very closely tied together in ancient Rome, and a sense of community was crucial. The point is not necessarily to tie family and business together like the Romans, merely that in our business pursuits we must not forsake family and community.

As for education, the Romans (especially the wealthy) began educating their children at about age seven, when primary school would cover the basics such as reading, writing, and arithmetic, as well as the traditional Roman faith, which reinforced moral values. At around age twelve, the most promising

---

[*] *Author's Note: Come to think of it, this is not unlike Twitter, where those with the most followers are viewed upon with envy.*

students (if their parents could afford it) would continue on to learn Greek and Latin literature, poetry, geography, history, Greek philosophy, and most importantly, the art of rhetoric (which was valuable for public persuasion or speaking in a court of law). Once reaching adulthood, education didn't stop there. In order for a soldier to move up through the ranks in the Roman military, education in engineering was necessary. Engineering was very much ingrained into the Roman military.

Likewise, we can become more well-rounded and vibrant by continuing to learn, not only in the field of project management, but in all areas of interest, and by offering our services, not only in the workplace and at home, but to the community and the world.

To summarize our lesson:

> Balance your key roles in life, and never forget the importance of family when setting your priorities. When mingling with your team, be sure to ask about their families to foster this mentality. Improve and renew yourself by making time for reading, exercise, public service, education, and any other hobbies of interest. Encourage your team to do the same.

CHAPTER FOUR

Pragmatic Innovation

True innovation must have a purpose. As comedian Sid Caesar (no relation to Julius) said, "The guy who invented the wheel was an idiot. The guy who invented the other three, he was a genius." The Romans are well known for their innovative engineering. But their innovations focused on practical needs. For instance, let's look at some examples from David Macaulay's definitive book, *City – A Story of Roman Planning and Construction.*

- Surveyors marked off roads using an instrument called a groma (a pole about four feet high on top of which a cross was laid flat). This was to ensure all roads intersected at right angles. A simple tool, created to fill a practical need.

- In order to saw hard stones needed for building, sand and steel filings were placed under a saw with a toothless blade to grind away the stone. If that didn't work, a row of holes was drilled where the stone was to be

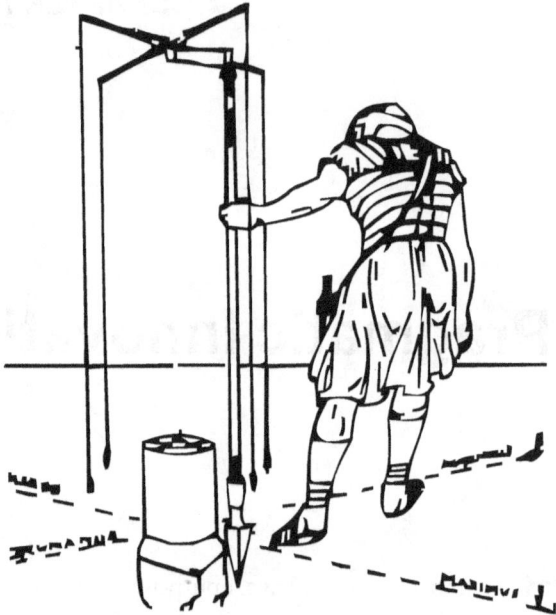

Figure 4.1 - Roman soldiers used the groma to lay out roads and building foundations.

divided. Wooden stakes were then jammed into the holes. When water was poured over the stakes, they swelled, splitting the stone along the line of holes.

- Knowing that wells would not be sufficient to supply water to a large population, a pipeline called an aqueduct was created to bring water from mountain lakes as far as 40 miles away (or longer). The aqueducts, each typically named for the person who led its construction, had to be built with a constant slope from beginning to end to keep the water moving. Some aqueducts were built above ground (it is surprising to some people that only 10 percent of Rome's aqueducts were above ground). To prevent people from stealing or poisoning the water, most of these above-ground aqueducts were raised about fifty feet off the ground. They were supported by a continuous row of arches built on tall square piers, which rested on deep foundations. The route chosen for the aqueduct sometimes required that a short tunnel be dug through a hill.

- Toilets were connected to sewer pipes and flushed by a continuous stream of water. This is especially interesting, since as late as the 1800's, people were still using chamber pots. That's because after the fall of Rome in 410 AD, the barbarians pretty much destroyed everything, and when Rome was later under Papal leadership, bathing and cleanliness was considered sinful and materialistic, and scientific exploration was considered an affront to God. As a result of the oppression during the Dark Ages and Middle ages, "modern plumbing" was lost for nearly 1,500 years, though some examples still remain (even though they were neglected for centuries). It wasn't until 1848, after a cholera epidemic was tied to stagnant water, that England passed the national Public Health Act, which required sanitary arrangements in every home. Around this time, the predecessor to the modern toilet was reinvented (not by Thomas Crapper, as some believe, but by Alexander Cumming, whose model was loosely based on an exclusive invention that Sir John Harrington created for his godmother, Queen Elizabeth I, some 200 years earlier).

It is worth noting that many of these innovations weren't for the purpose of increasing profits. The Romans didn't care about the ROI (Return on Investment) of their plumbing and other such initiatives. This was a matter of lifestyle, culture, and growth. Yet all of these inventions undoubtedly increased the wealth of Rome, both monetarily and as a society. Innovations do not have to be completely new inventions either. Many of the above mentioned innovations were not invented by the Romans, merely taken to new heights or put to new uses.

The ancient Egyptians had aqueducts (so did the Assyrians in 700 BC, but they used them to wage war and cause flooding against the Babylonians). The ancient Greeks had hot and cold showers and used baths for healing, and even an ancient Minoan Palace had a flushing toilet that led to sewers, as early as 1700 BC.

It was the Romans, however, that introduced plumbing on an unprecedented scale. The Romans introduced hot water boilers with hot and cold delivery systems. They "reinvented" flushable toilets by studying historic best practices (in all, the toilet was invented at least three times). They had complex gated systems to control the flow of water in their cities. They took aqueducts to a new scale. At its height, Rome had 11 public baths, nearly 1400 public fountains, and nearly 900 private baths (it's worth noting that the glory and status of Rome and the social aspects of bathing were considered essential and therefore qualified as a practical need).

These lessons in pragmatic creativity can serve us today as well. Today, we often add unexpected embellishments to make a product richer or more feature filled or to stand out from the pack. These extra features are fine in and of themselves. In fact, when developing a product for the market, this "wow" factor can serve to differentiate a product and delight the customer. In this sense, it's innovative and serves a purpose. But when designers or developers add these "surprise" features without regard for budget or scope, and without the input of the customer, problems can arise. Typically this is because it can add extra cost and may not even be desired by the customer. It's sort of like taxation without representation.

Of course, if a developer discovers well into the project, as sometimes happens, that a certain added feature would be of benefit to the customer or would delight the customer, there is nothing wrong with the project team agreeing to include the item if it does not add cost. Where possible, it's best to conduct research or ask the customer. This is an art more than a science. If it turns out the item would indeed increase the project's duration or cost (or the cost of the resulting product, if applicable), or if it will alter the expected outcome, then it's time to submit it as a change request for approval by management and/or the customer, if appropriate. The Walt Disney Company has a concept they call "little Wows"—those little inexpensive (or zero cost) items or services that can delight a customer. They've discovered that small, inexpensive surprises can have a large impact on customer perception. And let's face it; perception is reality.

Innovation also refers to the way project activities are performed. Team members should always be encouraged to contribute any insights or new groundbreaking methods that can achieve a goal quicker, better, or less costly. They should be encouraged to question current thinking or the status quo. They should be encouraged to work together and, if necessary, form their own sub-teams to develop solutions to problems, experimenting with various alternatives as necessary. Their ideas should be listened to, and they should be recognized for their innovations. Most Roman innovations came from their engineers, not from their leaders. They had a *culture of innovation*. We need to encourage this as well.

All in all, our takeaway from the Romans is:

> Encourage innovation, but innovate to fill a practical need. Consider small, inexpensive improvements that will delight the customer. Have a formal change management review if the innovations will alter the project's outcomes, duration, or cost. Encourage team participation in innovation. Challenge them to create new best practices that can accomplish the objective faster, less costly or more effectively (or better yet, all three). Finally, don't feel compelled to reinvent the wheel; seek far and wide for existing innovative practices, and improve upon them.

CHAPTER FIVE

Other Enabling Factors for Innovation

There were a number of other significant enablers for Roman innovation.

Staffing for Core Competencies

Engineering was, without a doubt, a core competency to the Romans, as evident in these excerpts from the well-researched Roman History, Coins and Technology Back Pages web site, selected as a Discovery Channel School valuable educational internet resource (http://www.jaysromanhistory.com/).

> "... In the applying of pure knowledge to practical uses, their engineers are unsurpassed until one reaches modern times. Engineers traveled with their

armies building roads and bridges. In fact, knowledge of engineering was almost a requirement for
advancing through the ranks. After they conquered
new territory and created a new province, their engineers laid out cities to a standard plan and provided
them with excellent roads and a clean water supply.
When Julius Caesar had to cross the Rhine with his
army, he built a pontoon bridge on the spot using the
engineering skills of his soldiers and forced labor of
the local tribesmen. Later, a much larger permanent
stone bridge crossed the Danube. They invented
concrete using pozzolana cement that would set
and harden underwater."

Rome became a great empire for many reasons: great
rulers, great armies, a suitable location, and notable achieve-
ments from visionary builders. It was the engineers, however,
that created the vast network of roads, bridges and aqueducts,
enabling Rome to achieve the growth that it did. Many of these
roads, bridges and aqueducts are still in use today. In fact, the
first aqueduct comparable in length to that of ancient Rome's
didn't happen until William Mulholland did it in 1913 with the
233-mile Los Angeles Aqueduct.

The Romans knew that engineering skills were needed,
not only to accomplish groundbreaking methods to support
the expanding population but also to enable their military to
accomplish what would not have been though possible without
those skills. This demonstrates not only that engineering was a
core competency but also reiterates our earlier point: the need
to apply innovations pragmatically; in this case, to support
population growth and military capability.

Figure 5.1 - Known as the Pont du Garde, this impressive Roman aqueduct still stands near Remoulins in the south of France.

Likewise, today's project managers should know the core competencies needed to accomplish their project's objectives, and should ensure that resources with those skills are obtained, or that existing resources are adequately trained. Many projects are bound by the limited skills of the resources at hand, and could benefit a great deal by innovations brought about by superior skills.

Let's retain this lesson regarding core competencies.

Know the core competencies needed to accomplish your objectives. Make sure your team is skilled in these competencies. Skill, knowledge and vision enable innovation.

Problems First; Solutions Second

We talked earlier about the pragmatic innovation. When we say
to innovate pragmatically, we are also implying an underlying
need to strive for problem-driven solutions. This is so uncom-
mon that to do so would be truly innovative. One good way
to ensure this is to consider the proposed product or enhancement from the end user's perspective—focusing first on the
situation before considering solutions. Geoffrey Moore, in
his book, *Crossing the Chasm*, talks about the need to develop
customer scenarios—that is, a written walkthrough of how
your customer (or end user) would use the product or enhancement, and how they operate now without it. Often, this
brings to light how useful the enhancement really would be,
and sometimes even identifies additional problems that need to
be addressed. Although Moore's book is for marketing new or
"disruptive" technology and applies this technique to judging
the marketability of a potential product, the same principle can
be very effective when analyzing a requested enhancement or
solution. It can also serve to ensure that the solution addresses
the problem holistically and effectively.

Let's examine how the need to address a problem was the
key driver for many projects of ancient Rome. For example,
the Romans expanded their network of roads primarily for military purposes—to allow an army to be quickly sent to trouble
spots as needed (they marked each mile [1,000 paces—or *mille*
in Latin] with a stone, giving us the word *milestone*). Their roads
also allowed for better trade and tax collection. Their aqueducts were built to bring water into the city because they knew
that wells could not support the population growth. Their sewage systems were designed to avoid floods, and disease caused

by stagnant waste. Water was delivered to homes through water mains, and was metered to enforce a tax on water use.

All of these creations were done because there was a problem that needed to be addressed. They did not start creating aqueducts because they saw examples in some ancient Mesopotamian texts and said, "Let's see what we can do with these." They did not undertake massive road building efforts just out of a desire to expand. Rather, they were done for military means and to enable more efficient tax collection. Even their circuses were created to solve a problem—to quiet the masses during the many periods of civil war.

Likewise, our projects (and the solutions they propose) should be undertaken to solve a problem. Hopefully, the project itself is already aligned with a corporate goal, ideally as part of a portfolio management system. Regardless, it is up to the project manager to ensure that this "problem-driven" approach filters down to the project team. Many organizations launch projects to implement a solution without a clear understanding of the problem the solution is meant to address. The project team then does its best to implement the solution successfully. But, because of the lack of understanding about the problem, the solution gets misused and sometimes abandoned.

Organizations also seem to enjoy reinventing the wheel. It is not necessary to create everything from scratch. The Romans, who did not have a strong Navy at the time of the Punic wars with the Carthaginians, captured a few Carthaginian ships during those wars. They were able to reverse engineer the ships, and as a result built a fleet of 200 ships in a few months' time. They created the strongest Navy in the world.

Figure 5.2 - Marble relief carving of a Roman naval vessel.

Let's pause to review the following lessons:

> Always ensure problem-driven solutions. Make sure the problem is clearly understood before proposing or implementing solutions. To perfectly implement a misguided solution serves nobody.

> To weigh the usefulness of a proposed enhancement, and to ensure problem-driven and client-centric solutions, try developing written customer scenarios that explain how the end user will use the solution. This may expose a lack of need, a better solution, or additional problems to solve.

> Don't reinvent the wheel. It wastes money and overlooks existing solutions. Many technological innovations of other ancient peoples only survive today because the Romans adopted them.

In summary, all of these elements of good engineering and design—innovating sensibly, fostering core competencies, and ensuring problem driven solutions—serve one ultimate purpose—to make the customer happy. Innovative solutions can delight the customer, especially if they result in shortening the project, lowering the cost, or providing a product that is extremely easy to use and easy to maintain. If you do come up with an idea that you think will improve the usability of the product, just be sure to confirm its usefulness with the customer and run the proposed change through the approval process if it will increase the project's scope, duration, or cost.

CHAPTER SIX

Planning and Risk Management

Not only were the Romans excellent engineers, as we have seen, but they were equally focused on the planning and risk management efforts necessary to ensure their ideas would come to fruition. They thought ahead and considered the "whole system" in their planning efforts. Again, let us reference David Macaulay's book, *City – A Story of Roman Planning and Construction*.

> "When cities were built, the maximum population and size were determined before construction began. The planners then allotted adequate space for houses, shops, squares and temples. They decided how much water would be needed and the number and size of streets, sidewalks and sewers.
>
> The planners agreed that when a city reached its maximum size, a new city would be built else-

where. They recognized the danger of overpopula-
tion. A city forced to grow beyond its walls not only
burdened the existing water, sewage and traffic
systems but eventually destroyed the farmland on
whose crops people depended."

Let's look at some specific examples of things that the Romans
did when planning a city, according to Macaulay's book:

- They selected a flat, sloping site (to ensure good drainage) that was high enough to avoid future floods

- Animal livers were examined to ensure that the environment was healthy, and the land was checked for
stagnant pools.

- They measured, designed and drew up a master plan
to allow for the agreed upon maximum population. A
copy of the plan was carved on marble and placed in
the forum for all to see.

- Planners planned for the location of the Forum (government and religious center), public water fountains,
aqueduct to bring in the water, central food market,
public baths and toilets, and an entertainment center
made up of a theater and amphitheater.

- Space was also set aside for future buildings.

- To ensure sunlight always reached the streets, no pri-
vately owned building could be higher than twice the
width of the street on which it stood.

- Aqueducts would bring water into the city from
faraway mountain lakes. The water would be gathered

in reservoirs and passed though gated, controlled, lead pipes to public fountains, toilets, and baths, or to homes of the wealthy. For drainage, sewers would carry excess water to tunnels, which led to the nearest river.

- The flow of water from the reservoirs was controlled via gates. When there was a shortage of water, the gates leading to homes of the wealthy were closed, and if necessary, the gates to the baths and toilets were closed as well. This ensured that the public fountains supplying the majority of the town's residents would be the last to run dry.

- Strict laws controlled any movement of carts and chariots that could endanger the health and safety of people in the streets. During the day, all carts and chariots except those carrying building materials were banned from the streets. Deliveries had to be made at night or early in the morning. To accommodate local homeowners or apartment dwellers, many streets were made one-way or dead-end to reduce the noisy traffic of carts and horses. Sidewalks on both sides of the streets were raised one and a half feet above the road surface to prevent vehicles from hitting pedestrians and to allow water to run through the streets into sewers during heavy rainfall.

From these examples, we can see that the Romans did considerable planning and exhaustively identified every possible known risk that could happen (and developed mitigation plans accordingly). They planned for disasters (whether it be floods, water shortage, or environmental problems). They planned for the future growth and long term maintainability (through space set aside for future buildings, and through their up front planning of the city's size—and the infrastructure to support it). They established laws and processes that would allow for maximum usability of the city (whether for safety, entertainment or comfort—for example, ensuring that sunlight hit the streets, or implementing traffic safety laws).

Disaster, growth, maintainability, and risks to usability should be part of every risk management plan. About the only thing I wouldn't recommend is putting your project plan in marble, as we now have tools like Microsoft Project and other project management software to be able to constantly adapt the plan to reality and the ever-changing environment. All evidence indicates that the Romans did not have these software products and therefore carved the plan in marble. One thing they did do right, however, is that they put the plan in a visible spot for all to see. Again, through the use of the Internet (or an intranet), there are other ways to do this today. For extremely large plans, wall charts are often used but to be effective they need to be replaced frequently. Most often, soon after a wall chart is put up, reality has already altered the plan.

For now, let's take note of this lesson:

> Plan extensively. Make sure your risk management plan allows for: disaster, growth, maintainability, and risks to usability. Project plans and risk management plans are dynamic and ever-changing, and should be reviewed, updated, and communicated throughout your project.

The Importance of Templates

We've discussed how the Romans engineered innovatively and pragmatically, and planned for all possible risks, but one additional thing they did was to create a standard template, which they used to create each and every city using a standard process. The Romans, if nothing else, were efficient. As we've seen, they did not like to reinvent the wheel, and this applied to their own processes as well.

Likewise, project managers should have template work breakdown structures and/or project plans for each type of project that they typically undertake. Whenever lessons learned are captured for a project (which ideally should be at each check-in, at planned stage gates, and at the end of the project), the next step should be to update the standard templates with any applicable changes as a result of the lessons learned.

Therefore, each standard template should be a working document, and be kept up to date as needed. If template ideas are needed, consult the Project Management Institute's *Practice Standard for Work Breakdown Structures*, available online from the PMI Bookstore. It's also worth mentioning that a template is just that – a template, or guide. It is not a project plan and is not a substitute for designing an effective work breakdown structure or project plan. It merely makes the job simpler, and saves time by providing standard deliverables and activities that need to be done for each project.

In summary:

> Make efficient use of repeatable processes through standard templates that are maintained regularly. Make the update of these templates (if necessary) an output of the lessons learned activity, which should be performed at checkpoints throughout the project and at the end of each project.

CHAPTER SEVEN

The Rise of the Roman Empire

Now that we've explored the principles and competencies that served as the foundation of ancient
Rome, we can examine its chronological history
within the right context. In order to keep the flow going, we
will first explore Rome's rise before reviewing the lessons,
though some of the lessons will be apparent (in fact, you may
even want to make notes of your own lessons throughout this
journey). We must review this history from a bird's eye view
of course, as we have many years to span. Then, once we've
reviewed Rome's rise and the lessons it brings, we'll explore its
decline and fall, and see what lessons we can derive from that.

Meanwhile, the "executive summary" version of Rome's
rise is that Rome started out as a monarchy, then became a
republic, and eventually became the greatest empire the world

had ever known. Now that we know that, let's explore how this happened.

The Early Monarchy Period

Although mired in myth, the agreed upon date of the foundation of Rome is 21 April 753 BC, when Romulus allegedly became its first king. As legend has it, Romulus had murdered his twin brother Remus after the two were arguing over who had the support of the local deities to rule the city. Romulus named the city Rome. To this day the Lupa Capitolina, a medieval bronze statue depicting Romulus and Remus as babies being nursed by a she-wolf, is recognized as the symbol of Rome. Some speculate that the wolf (lupa in Latin) represents the human priestesses of a fox goddess, which were also known as lupa.

Figure 7.1 - A coin bearing the image of King Romulus on one side and an image from the legend of Romulus and Remus on the other side.

Around this time, the Etruscans were the dominant tribe in Italy. They were based in an area of Italy called Etruria, and are believed to have come from Asia Minor (now Turkey). The entire plain, Latinium, upon which Rome was settled, was made up of various Latin tribes, but the more advanced Etruscans took over and became a dynasty. Various kings, for the most part Etruscans, succeeded Romulus, and continued to rule Rome until 509 BC, when Roman noblemen revolted. They were provoked when Lucretia, a Roman noblewoman, killed herself in shame after being raped by the son of the king. This resulted in the overthrow of the Etruscan monarchy.

It's worth noting that the Romans did end up benefiting from the Etruscans, as they inherited the ability to write (although the Etruscans wrote in Greek and the Romans wrote in Latin), as well as a slew of public buildings and knowledge in political and military organization.

The Republic of Rome

In 509 BC, following the overthrow of the Etruscan monarchy, the Republic of Rome was established. It was based on the Greek model, and was made up of the Senate (comprised of Rome's leading citizens who had governmental advisory roles in the past) and the people of Rome.

To this day, the abbreviation SPQR adorns many public buildings and statues of Rome and was engraved on the battle uniforms of the Roman legion. It stands for *senatus populusque romanus* and means "the senate and the people of Rome."

Expansion of the Republic

Over the next 200 years, the Romans expanded to most of the Italian peninsula. They fought off many wars against other allied Latin tribes, and had doubled in size, becoming the dominant Latin tribe. They were nearly destroyed when they were

Figure 7.2 - An example of the SPQR abbreviation from the ruins of Rome.

defeated and overthrown by the Gauls (predecessors of the French) in 387BC.

Ultimately, they recovered by improving their army, and constructing a wall around their seven hills, but most of all, by forming key strategic alliances. Through this, they were able to dominate northern and central Italy. Then, as word spread, various southern cities began to seek protection from the Romans. As a result, the Romans offered them alliances, and this led to the Romans dominating the whole of Italy.

The next thing the Romans did was to build roads and improve communications, which enabled the rapid spread of the Latin language and the Roman way of life. Later, the network of roads would be expanded to enable rapid military deployment to trouble areas, and to enable more efficient tax collection.

While Rome was now the most powerful force in Italy, the Western Mediterranean was under the control of Carthage, a city in North Africa. With Carthage moving in ever closer to Roman territory, and thus causing a threat to the southern Greek villages under Roman protection, the Punic Wars began (264 – 146 BC). This led to the defeat of the Carthaginians (including the otherwise brilliant Carthaginian general, Hannibal), and eventually the Roman acquisition of Sicily, Sardinia and Corsica. Ultimately, even Greece fell to the Romans, giving Rome control of the entire Mediterranean. Regarding Hannibal, the legendary Carthaginian commander, his strategic insights and methods were so effective that the Romans began to adopt them in their own military. He is considered to this day among the greatest military strategists of all time.

After these wars, in came the treasures and captured slaves, bringing prosperity and, paradoxically, poverty, as the rich got richer and the poor got poorer. The independent farmers sold their land to the increasingly prosperous rich, who used captured slaves for cheap labor instead of the working class.[*]

Meanwhile, the Senate pacified the working class by feeding them bread and entertaining them with circuses. The few tribunes who challenged this exploitative system were quickly quieted.

---

[*] *As a side note, this is not unlike what is happening today, with mega-corporations and developers overtaking or absorbing small businesses, and work being outsourced to cheap labor to cut costs.*

Military Leadership and Dictatorship

What followed was an inevitable period of rebellion and civil war, which led to a series of army commanders taking over control of Rome. This was exacerbated by the fact that the Roman government was struggling to deal with their increasing remote territories, as a result of Rome's rapid expansion. The Senate eventually responded with Sulla, a rival general of their own. Sulla was described as having the cunning of a fox and the courage of a lion, a combination that Machiavelli later described as the ideal characteristics of a ruler. This was just what was needed during such turbulent times. He also made reforms to the Roman constitution to restore the balance of power between the Senate and the Tribunate (elected officials). Eventually, however, Sulla fell to the trappings of power, becoming a dictator and destroying the Senate and the Republic along with it. Once again, this led to a period of Civil war—the very thing Sulla was brought in to stop. Ultimately, Sulla came to his senses and in 81 BC he resigned his dictatorship and disbanded his legions.

Figure 7.3 - Lucius Cornelius Sulla (135-78 BCE)

Spartacus and the Uprising of the Masses

In 73 BC, a revolt almost succeeded when a gladiator, Spartacus, quite effectively led 70,000 slaves and dispossessed farmers in a major uprising. This was gloriously depicted in Stanley Kubric's film, *Spartacus*, with Kirk Douglas in the lead role.

The revolt was eventually put down by Crassus (played by Sir Laurence Olivier in the film), who was appointed by the Senate to stop the rebellion. As a result, 6,000 of Spartacus's followers were crucified. In the film, Spartacus is crucified along with his men, although in real life he was never found. The last anybody saw of him, he was fighting valiantly with a spear in his knee.

During this time, civil war and unrest persisted. Attempting to calm things down, Sulla's successor, Pompey the Great, joined forces with Crassus and another military man, Julius Caesar. Together they formed a triumvirate, known as the First Triumvirate, a powerful ruling body meant to prevent another dictator like Sulla from taking over.

Figure 7.4 - The Triumvirate: Gaius Julius Caesar, Marcus Licinius Crassus, and Gnaeus Pompeius Magnus.

Caesar, Antony, and Cleopatra

When Crassus died, Pompey and Caesar quarreled over politics. Pompey, a conservative, favored aristocracy, limiting the power of the popular assemblies (ordinary citizens who served as the legislative branch) and tribunes (elected officials), and extending power to the Senate. Caesar, the popularist, who favored the rights of the people, opposed this. After campaigns in Northern Europe, Caesar brought his troops back to Rome, brazenly crossing the Rubicon River in defiance of the Senate's wishes. According to Roman law, a military leader wasn't allowed to bring his troops too close to Rome (a law meant to prevent another Sulla). Caesar knew that this would put him in a precarious position with Pompey, and that this could decide the fate of Rome's future. Many view Caesar's crossing of the Rubicon, in which he famously stated "the die is cast," as a turning point in Roman history, and the event that enabled Rome's ultimate expansion as an empire. In response to Caesar's bold move, Pompey took his army and most of the Senate to Greece. While Pompey was planning an attack on Caesar, Caesar made a successful preemptive strike on Pompey. Caesar returned to Rome in triumph.

The rioting stopped and the Senate was gradually behind him (at least publicly). Caesar brought much needed order to Rome, and passed laws to relieve financial hardship and reduce debts. He improved the administration, bringing a period of political and financial stability, and was a passionate builder (all of this would serve to inspire Napoleon approximately 1,800 years later). With all this, he was creating the foundation that would lead to Rome's unprecedented growth. As a result of his successes and popularity, he was made dictator for life. Unfortunately, this was his undoing.

Over time, Caesar grew more narcissistic, envisioning himself as a god, and acting without the Senate. As a result, a conspiracy formed against him and he was eventually killed, stabbed 23 times on March 15, 44 BC (the Ides of March).

Figure 7.5 - The famous Roman coin minted by Brutus and Cassius, celebrating the death of Caesar.

After Caesar's death, Civil War resumed, as people jockeyed for position. That came to an end when Marc Antony, Caesar's co-consul, and Octavian, Caesar's grand-nephew and adopted son, collaborated with an army leader, Lepidus to form the Second Triumvirate. This collaboration didn't last, as Antony rejected his wife, Octavian's sister, for Cleopatra, the Egyptian Queen. Angered, Octavian (with the Senate's backing) declared war on Antony. Sensing inevitable defeat, Antony and Cleopatra committed suicide, leaving Octavian to rule Rome.

Figure 7.6 - Gaius Julius Caesar Octavianus (known as Augustus) became the first Roman Emperor.

From Republic to Empire

Octavian now triumphant, became the true first emperor of Rome in 27 BC, and was soon named Augustus (meaning "the revered one") by the Senate.

Augustus was an anomaly. In his earlier days as part of the Second Triumvirate, he was extremely shrewd, and often gained obedience through brutal means. He was also somewhat unforgiving. According to Suetonius (in his book, *The Twelve Caesars*) he once had a knight stabbed and killed just for taking notes at a speech he was addressing to a soldiers' assembly. He thought the note taking was perhaps suspicious. During this time, many such acts won him the hatred of the people.

Ironically, he would eventually be remembered for his leniency and fairness, the most revered emperor of all, and he later regretted many of his prior actions. Of course, whether he was truly transformed (perhaps as a result of several alleged health scares) or whether this was all part of his plan for winning over the people, only Augustus knows for sure. Most historians seem to think it was a sincere transformation.

What we do know about Augustus is that he appeared to be extremely goal oriented. During the Triumvirate years, he needed to use strong discipline to bring order out of chaos, much like Caesar before him. (Remember, these were times of rebellion and civil war.) Later, he needed to win over the Senate and the people, as he was astute enough to realize he wouldn't get far otherwise. After that, he needed to establish an administrative bureaucracy to accommodate the already huge empire (including adding a larger forum to accommodate the increasing number of lawsuits due to the expanding population). Augustus was perhaps the ultimate situational leader and was able to adapt to changing needs.

He was also smart enough to realize that they needed to put a halt to expansion for now and that they should instead concentrate on increasing security along the existing borders. That said, he did expand the empire quite as bit through battles with warring barbarian tribes, yet even then he was reported to have never attacked a city needlessly, and was able to maintain peace in the conquered lands through peace treaties and fair treatment of the inhabitants. This reputation of leniency and fairness actually triggered other nations to come to Augustus offering peace agreements.

Augustus also concentrated heavily on security, both his own and that of the Roman Empire. He boosted his own security by cutting the number of legions, paying off retired soldiers, and surrounding himself with a highly-paid imperial guard (called the Praetorian Guard). Ironically, it was these guards who would eventually gain more power than some of the future emperors. He boosted the security of the empire by firming up the borders and undertaking projects to make Rome less vulnerable to fire and river floods.

Figure 8.1 - A marble relief of the Praetorian Guard.

Augustus wanted, more than anything, to make a lasting difference, as evident in his own words (as documented by Suetonius):

> "May I be privileged to build firm and lasting foundations for the Government of the State. May I also achieve the reward to which I aspire: that of being known as the author of the best possible Constitution, and of carrying with me, when I die, the hope that these foundations which I have established for the State will abide secure."

He wanted to make a lasting difference, and indeed he had.

Unlike his uncle before him, Augustus took care not to offend the Senate. He even offered at one time to restore Rome to the Senate and the people (i.e. the old Republic). However, it was an offer that he knew the Senate couldn't accept (which was why he offered it). The result was that he was revered for having made the offer in the first place.

What helped matters was that Augustus lived and dressed simply, and was not gratuitous in his display of power. He preferred the food of the common people and was a habitually light drinker. He preferred to rule from behind the scenes while allowing the Senate to function externally. This proved to be very effective, and won the trust of the Senate and the people.

He included both noblemen and the working class in his administration. Art and literature also flourished during this period, as Augustus encouraged intellectual exploration. He even wrote a book (one of many that he authored) called, *An Encouragement to the Study of Philosophy*. Also, a massive rebuilding effort was undertaken to effectively portray Rome as the super power that it was. Augustus claimed that he transformed Rome from a city of brick to a city of marble, and indeed he had.

In addition to rebuilding the city, Augustus worked to rebuild the character of the people as well. He instituted laws that prohibited young people from attending evening games without an adult. His laws particularly focused on matters that dealt with adultery and bribery, and he encouraged marriage, at least in the higher ranks. As Suetonius pointed out, he also cleaned up the town by eliminating organized crime (yes, they had it then, too) and stationing armed police in bandit-ridden districts. He also restored public buildings erected by honorable men of the past. According to Suetonius, he then proclaimed:

> "This has been done to make my fellow citizens insist that both I (while I am alive), and my successors, shall not fall below the standard set by those great men of old."

Augustus became known for his patience and tolerance (a far cry from his early days). He discouraged rashness, and even had a favorite saying, "Make haste slowly."

He encouraged independence of mind and vetoed a law that would have suppressed free speech. He was known as a man of the people, and often visited the sick and appeared in courts. He even had his Forum made narrower than planned because he refused to have civilians' homes demolished to make room for the originally proposed larger one.

As a result of his integrity and his actions, in the end, Augustus was remembered for leading with competency and compassion. His reforms resulted in a time of relative peace and prosperity during his 41 years reign and for 150 years thereafter, despite Rome's share of bad rulers. This time, which spanned nearly 200 years, was called the Pax Romana, or Roman peace.

A Roman Peace – Sort of

During the so-called Pax Romana, things were not always as rosy as the phrase would indicate. For every decent emperor there were several extremely corrupt ones.

Augustus' stepson, Tiberius, started out with good intentions, but was not as effective a manager as Augustus. He then began displaying excesses that even rivaled his more infamous successor, Caligula. Even Caligula started out somewhat normal for a few months, until mental illness apparently took hold and led him down his infamous path of extreme cruelty and debauchery.

After Caligula was murdered, Claudius, the grandson of Augustus, became emperor. Although he was assumed by many to be unfit for the job (he stuttered and was slightly crippled), he turned out to be a good and steady ruler. He introduced civil service reforms and expanded the Roman Empire to include Britain. Nero also started out somewhat normal, and then became violent and excessive (he eventually committed suicide after being declared a public enemy by the Senate).

Why did so many emperors begin with good intentions, yet end up so corrupt and excessive? Perhaps Abraham Lincoln said it best when he said, "Nearly all men can stand adversity, but if you want to test a man's character, give him power." Very few passed this test.

After this period followed a series of three pretty inept emperors, two mediocre ones, and a horrible one. The first two were chosen and then killed and replaced at will by the Praetorian Guard, which if you recall was created by Augustus to

Figure 8.2 - Tiberius Claudius Caesar Augustus Germanicus ("Claudius") the fourth Roman Emperor.

protect the emperor. The third, Vitellius, was a general chosen by the legions on the Rhine River. Finally, not at all happy with Vitellius, the legions on the Danube River chose their own general, Vespasian, to be emperor. Vespasian killed Vitellius and became the next emperor.

During this time there were several uprisings, including a major one in Judea (the Roman word for Judah, the southern Jewish kingdom of which Jerusalem was the capital). Vespasian's first mission was to quell the uprisings (a task he was originally charged with as a general under Nero). In the end, he had his son, Titus (who would later become his successor), do the dirty work, destroying the Jewish Second Temple in Jerusalem in 70 AD (the first being the Temple of Solomon, part of which survives to this day as the Western Wall).

Judea was a thorn in Rome's side since the days of Nero. There were rumors, ultimately unsubstantiated, that prophets predicted that out of Judea would come the next ruler of the world. Therefore, the destruction of the temple was a major event, commemorated by the Arch of Titus in Rome, which bears the words "Judea Capta" (Judea has been conquered). The Romans even created their own cheer, "Hip! Hip!" which is an acronym for *Hierosolyma Est Perdita* (or "Jerusalem is gone"). Gone it was, at least for then.

All in all, Vespasian was remembered as a practical and capable emperor, as he restored order to the empire, especially in the outlying provinces, where he gave the people citizenship. He also restored political and financial stability (despite some financial improprieties of his own) and was an avid builder (including the Colosseum, which was eventually completed by Titus). His major vice, as reported by Suetonius, was greed, as he raised taxes considerably, and often used the funds for disreputable purposes.

Figure 8.3 -Imperator Caesar Vespasianus Augustus.

His son, Titus, succeeded him and surprisingly (considering his brutal reputation in the past) ended up being a compassionate and fair leader, devoting much of his time organizing public relief efforts after a plague swept though the Italian peninsula. He died after only two years in office, leaving us with these intriguing last words: "I have made only one mistake."

The last emperor in the Flavian Dynasty (named for Vespasian, whose full name was Titus Flavius Vespasianus) was Domitian, Titus's younger brother. He alienated the Senate, ruled as a tyrant, and was basically hated by everyone. He was assassinated in 96 AD.

The Five Good Emperors

Nearly 70 years after Augustus became the first emperor of Rome, there was finally a long string of five good emperors from the years 96 to 180 AD, a span of nearly 100 years (later, the Romans would imaginatively refer to them as "The Five Good Emperors"). This is not to say that these were the only good emperors, or that they were perfect (they all had some faults), merely that this was the first time in Rome's long history, that there was such a long succession of decent emperors.

The first of these emperors was Nerva, a lawyer chosen by the Senate (after Domitian's tyrannical reign, the Senate wisely knew that a trusted and capable emperor was needed). It was Nerva who instituted the policy of an emperor choosing his successor. The successor, until becoming Emperor, would retain the title of "Caesar" (incidentally, the source of the later titles "Kaiser" and "Czar" used by the Germans and Russians, respectively). When the successor became Emperor, the title would switch to "Augustus." Therefore, when an emperor chose his successor, he would make him Caesar.

The remaining "good" emperors were Trajan, Hadrian, Antoninus Pius, and Marcus Aurelius (played by Richard Harris in the film, *Gladiator*). All five, beginning with Nerva, were educated, interested in philosophy, devoted to their duties, and loved by the people.

Trajan ruled effectively for twenty years, establishing good relations with the Senate, building extensively, and most of all, expanding the empire through military conquests of Eastern Europe. He ultimately expanded the Roman border all the way to the Persian Gulf. His one critical failing was his intense desire to expand, which led to many revolts from all sides.

Hadrian succeeded Trajan, and adopted a more Augustan approach by establishing a non-expansionist policy. Instead he concentrated on firming up security on the borders (building the now famous Hadrian's Wall between England and Scotland), and even gave up some of Trajan's conquests in the east. He also cleaned up some of the political and financial messes left behind by Trajan's policies and endeavors. He introduced a number of legal, civil and administrative reforms. Ironically, in the end, he was not as popular as Trajan (except perhaps by the soldiers), possibly because of his cantankerous manner.

Antoninus Pius succeeded Hadrian, and had a reputation for being fair, mild-mannered, and humble. He ruled for 23 years and introduced a number of legal reforms, including the presumption of innocence until proven guilty. He one failing was his lack of military focus, which led to some weaknesses along the borders, where there was increasing threat of rebellion.

The last, and possibly the most revered of the Five Good Emperors, was Marcus Aurelius. He was dignified, introspective and devoted. He was a pacifist who preferred writing to warfare (his most famous work being his collective philosophical journals known as *Meditations*). Unfortunately, he inherited the constant threats at the borders from barbarian tribes, and spent much of his time trying to keep them out. So, in a way, he was a reluctant warrior. It was to his credit that he held the empire together for as long as he did (which was 19 years).

His biggest mistake was naming his son, Commodus, to be the next emperor (as the trend had previously, and successfully, shifted from hereditary succession to choosing who would be most effective). This would prove to be an unwise decision. When Marcus Aurelius died, his last words to his friends were "Go to the rising sun; mine is setting." Unfortunately, so was that of the Roman Empire.

Figure 8.4 - Marcus Aurelius Antoninus Augustus was the last of the Five Good Emperors and an important stoic philosopher.

CHAPTER NINE

Lessons Learned from Rome's Ascendance

Although we've referred to our history so far as *the rise of Rome*, as we can see, there were really many rises and falls (just as there are with any corporation). All in all, however, despite the ups and downs, Rome was growing during that time (which is more than can be said for its decline), and the excesses of the odd emperor didn't typically impact the average person. So, from a very high level, we can consider this "the rise."

So, what do we know so far about how Rome went from monarchy to republic to the largest empire the world had ever known? What led to its greatest successes during those thousand years?

We already know that they tied all of their objectives to one overall goal□ satisfying the gods' wishes that they extend their form of civilization to the rest of the world. We know that they inspired loyalty by positioning their objectives as being preferable to the alternatives of tyranny or barbarism. We know that they valued obedience, although sometimes had brutal ways of ensuring it (today there are better ways, and even some of the Roman emperors were more enlightened than others).

We also know that they valued family and education, to make people well rounded and balanced, and to improve society as whole. Finally, we know that they fostered engineering as a core competency, and that they were innovative, yet problem-driven, practical and efficient. They did not like to reinvent the wheel and were not above copying from others.

What other lessons have we picked up in our brief tour of the rise of the Roman Empire? To be sure, people did not accept absolute leaders or monarchy. This is what led the monarchy to become a republic. Caesar certainly was capable and gained power through his strategic and tactical skills, yet when he essentially became dictator, this led to his demise (as it had later with Caligula and Nero). He simply upset too many people.

This is a lesson that he should have learned from the initial rise of the republic to begin with. The republic expanded by developing strategic alliances. Of course, their military capability helped, but they could not have expanded so broadly and rapidly without making such alliances. This ability to focus on strong alliances was a common element of all of Rome's successful leaders, from the early republic to Augustus to the Five Good Emperors.

There are several elements to making strong and strategic alliances. The word "strategic" is the key. Certainly, building relationships and networking are a crucial part of any alliance. However, to make a strategic alliance, one must know what kind of alliance is needed at what time and with whom. Once again, I'll refer to Geoffrey Moore's excellent book, *Crossing the Chasm*, which details how to target the appropriate audience at the appropriate time when planning a high-tech product launch. A similar technique can be used to build the alliances needed to ensure project success.

Moore refers to the different stages of adoption of a high-tech product as the "technical adoption lifecycle." In this lifecycle, there are five levels of adoption: the *techies* (who are fanatically in favor of your endeavor), the *visionaries* (who are early adopters, and thus your champions, with their own agendas that your endeavor just happens to support), the *pragmatics* (or early majority, who are generally open to new things, but must see a practical use for them), the *conservatives* (or late majority, who are against change in general, but will accept it if the early majority does and they have no other choice), and finally the *skeptics* (who are extremely opposed to your endeavor, and although you can learn from their concerns, they can potentially be a barrier).

The primary difference between marketing an idea and building alliances for your project is that of timing. With your project, you'll most likely want to consider all of the above audiences very early in your project. When marketing a product (especially a niche or high-tech one), these audiences need to be approached in sequence and at the right time. The bottom line is that, when building alliances, it's important to recognize that the above audiences exist, and that they all have different concerns and therefore should not be approached the same way.

Moore also refers to the need to build a strong "invasion force," by securing alliances with strategic suppliers and partners that can strengthen your cause and ensure success.

What this all means to the project manager is that by identifying and categorizing your stakeholders, addressing their needs appropriate to their concerns, and allying yourself with the right vendors and relevant peer functional groups (i.e. external and internal partners), you can effectively build strategic alliances.

Finally, Moore suggests determining your product's niche, which adds much needed focus for both the development team and the potential customer (we spoke of positioning earlier, which helps achieve this focus). In a sense, this focus (which the project manager must strive to provide) helps make your team a strong partner in the alliance.

To summarize our point about strategic alliances, which was a key enabling factor in the rise of the Roman Republic:

> Make strategic alliances with suppliers, relevant functional groups, and all stakeholders (including the customer and your team). When marketing your project, be considerate of your stakeholders' perspective and their concerns. Be sure to make strong alliances with your project team by providing the project's reason for being.

Throughout Rome's rise, there were a number of excellent leaders from whom we can learn, and a fair share of bad ones. Without a doubt, it was Augustus who made the greatest impact on the rise of Rome, building on the foundation laid by Caesar. Augustus's legacy was so lasting that even the occasional rise of an incredibly corrupt emperor was not enough to destroy it.

What did Augustus and the relatively few successful emperors who followed have in common that separated them from the pack? In addition to building strategic alliances (which they certainly had in common), I have identified five additional elements that led to their success.

1. Leading from Behind the Scenes

For one, they all led from behind the scenes while allowing the Senate to flourish. In other words, they adopted a win-win philosophy. In Joel R. DeLuca's excellent book, *Political Savvy - Systematic Approaches to Leadership Behind-the-Scenes*, he describes this win-win approach as the most effective style of leadership and politics today. The least effective is the "Machiavellian" style; one who assumes that organizational life is a win-lose proposition.

This doesn't mean that project managers should sit in the background and just let things happen. It merely means that project managers must not make decisions or judgments in isolation, and must consider the impact on all stakeholders, be it the team, management, the customer, or the organization. They must also consider the impact on the future: how their decision will impact the product after the project has been completed. This holistic approach is what Geoffrey Moore refers to in his book as "Whole Product Marketing"☐ the need to consider all impacts when developing and marketing a product. In my book, *Managing the Gray Areas*, I talk about the importance of systems thinking; examining all variables that can impact an outcome, as well as their relationships to one another; this is fundamentally the same concept.

Another element of leading behind the scenes is that project managers should not take sole credit for their team's accomplishments. Several renowned sages of the past have said that a great leader should always give credit to his people for success and always absorb the blame for failure. Wise advise indeed.

2. Ongoing Skills Development

The second thing that all of these emperors had in common was that they were students of their craft; they were educated, interested in philosophy, and devoted to their duties. This does not mean that you need to have a doctorate in philosophy to be successful, merely that those who are introspective, continuously learning, and are open to different ways of doing things, tend to be most effective. This goes back to Stephen Covey' seventh habit of success, "sharpening your saw," as we discussed earlier.

3. Leading with Competency and Compassion

Third, all of these leaders led with competency and compassion. That is, they were organized; they adhered to principles of good management and leadership; they empathized with the needs of their subordinates and all stakeholders; and they did not isolate themselves from their staff by being extravagant or abusing their power. This is a good recipe for success for any leader.

4. Being Goal Oriented

Fourth, they were all goal oriented and were able to adapt their approach to the situation at hand. Augustus initially inherited a chaotic and war-torn situation and therefore needed to begin by instilling discipline. (Of course, his youth also brought along some brutal approaches to this). Once order resumed, his goal changed to building alliances necessary for security and stability. He also needed to install an administrative infrastructure capable of effectively managing such an enormous empire. As he grew older, his goal changed to ensuring lasting changes beyond his reign, and he did this by rebuilding the city, rebuilding the very character of the people of Rome, and establishing laws and reforms that would ensure stability for years to come.

Project managers can learn from this by understanding the situation with which they are faced; for example, streamlining (and even eliminating) bureaucracy when faced with extreme situations. Keep in mind that, in normal situations, some bureaucracy (i.e. official procedure) is needed but never unnecessary bureaucracy. Administrative tasks should always be re-examined for their need.

5. Promoting Transformational Change

Finally, all of these leaders (and especially Augustus) understood transformational change and were able to introduce
new paradigms, new ways of thinking. They instituted needed
reforms, not just for change's sake, but because they were ob-
servant enough to see a need for change, and understood how
to introduce it correctly. For more on transformational change,
I recommend Dean Anderson and Linda Ackerman Ander-
son's book, *Beyond Change Management* (as well as its partner, *The
Change Leader's Roadmap*). Both books are available at http://
www.beingfirst.com/.

According to the authors, transformational change requires
an understanding of the "human, cultural and change process
dynamics" that are at play in any major transformation. As part
of their approach, the authors suggest looking for a "WIN-
win-win" solution, or an "Enterprise Win-Win." This relates
to our earlier analogy of "whole product marketing" and the
importance of considering all impacts and perspectives.

Let's recap our five additional lessons from Augustus and
other great Roman emperors:

Lead from behind the scenes. Always look for win-win solutions. Always give your team the credit for successes and
absorb the blame for failures.

Never stop learning and always keep an open mind.

Lead with competency and compassion. Be organizationally
aware, study effective leadership techniques, and empathize
with your stakeholders.

Be goal-oriented and adaptive. Use the right tools for the job at hand. Install organizational administration to bring order out of chaos. Eliminate bureaucracy when faced with extreme situations. Always try to keep bureaucracy to its smallest effective format.

Especially for large projects, make it a point to study transformational change management. Don't expect buy-in or dedication from people unless you have studied and know how to apply the techniques required for successful transformational change.

CHAPTER TEN

The Decline and Fall of the Roman Empire

Ve've explored the principles and elements that led to the rise of the Roman Empire and have applied these lessons to modern day project management. Now let's examine the decline of the Roman Empire and see what lessons we can learn.

If you recall, the last good Emperor that the Romans had was Marcus Aurelius (ably portrayed by Richard Harris in the film, *Gladiator*). After the death of Marcus Aurelius in 180 AD, everything went downhill. A string of mostly bad emperors followed, beginning with Commodus (played by Joachin

Phoenix in the film, *Gladiator*, although the film was only partly factual). After Commodus (and after two very short-lived and completely inept emperors, Pertinax and Didius Julianus), the mostly poor-to-mediocre Severan Dynasty ruled for about 50 years (including the Emperor Caracalla, known mostly for his extravagant public baths and spas).

The important thing is that during all this time, with constant threats along the perimeter of the empire, power was shifting from Rome to the Roman provinces responsible for defense along the borders. This eventually led to a period of military generals from these provinces taking control (the so-called "barracks emperors"). Civil wars alone nearly tore apart the empire, as various army factions nominated and backed their own rulers. For 30 years, there was a pattern of generals becoming emperor, and then being murdered to make way for another. To make matters worse, economy was weak as well.

Splitting Heirs

Fortunately, in 284 AD, Diocletian, the last of the barracks emperors (but much more effective than the ones before him), finally made reforms that once again brought order to the empire. He enlarged the army and gave them power of administration. He increased security, and restored stability after years of civil war. Unfortunately, he also shared the narcissistic tendencies of Caesar and began to perceive himself as a deity. In addition, he ended up raising taxes considerably to fund the large army and resources to support it. This, combined with the poor economy, caused much dissention among the masses.

In 286 AD, he made what many feel to be the first mistake that ultimately led to the fall of the empire (there were several more made by others). He decided that since Rome had grown so large and unmanageable, it should be divided into an Eastern and Western Empire. Ultimately, he divided the empire even further, with four co-emperors each of whom had a quarter of the empire with its own administration center. While the idea had merit, this was a fatal mistake and was the beginning of the end as conflict would inevitably follow. Abraham Lincoln was right when he said, "A house divided cannot stand." What made matters worse was that Diocletian wasn't up to the task of overseeing this transition and creating the right structure to integrate the overall empire. What resulted was the largest bureaucracy known to man, a complex administrative nightmare.

Figure 10.1 - Gaius Aurelius Valerius Diocletianus was the first Roman Emperor to voluntarily remove himself from office.

Constantine, and the Rise of Constantinople

Ultimately, conflicts did indeed arise between rulers of the separate quadrants of the Roman Empire. In the east, two emperors fought for supremacy (Licinius and Maximinus Daia), and in the west, two others fought (Constantine and Maxentius). In the west, in 312, Constantine invaded Rome, defeating Maxentius's much larger army. On his way to Rome, Constantine claimed he saw the *Chi-Ro* (a monogram that represented the symbol of Christ) in the sun, and thus had his soldiers paint the symbol on their shields. He credited his unlikely victory to the power of Christ and from that point on embraced Christianity. Meanwhile, in the east, Licinius defeated Maximinus II Daia a year later. This left only two emperors, Constantine in the west and Licinius in the east.

Figure 10.2 - Gaius Flavius Valerius Aurelius Constantinus.

In 315, Licinius spearheaded a revolt against Constantine. A year later, Constantine attacked and defeated Licinius. Battles persisted, many due to religious debates, until 324, when Constantine defeated Licinius once and for all, having him imprisoned and eventually executed. Constantine was now the undisputed emperor.

As emperor, Constantine continued and furthered the military and administrative reforms started by Diocletian (and unfortunately the associated taxes as well). He improved security and built lavishly, recalling some of the old glory of Rome at its peak. In many ways, he was Rome's last great emperor. In fact, one would be hard pressed to name any emperors that followed. However, his most lasting achievement was that he ruled as a Christian (whereas Christians were persecuted under Diocletian's rule), establishing Christianity as the official religion of Rome and thus the Western world. Christianity had been spreading through Rome since the days of Nero, but it was now official. Ironically, Rome had gone from the place that killed its Christians to the seat of the Church and the seed of the growth of Christianity. Despite his role in endorsing and expanding Christianity, however, Constantine remained tolerant of other religions, including Paganism.

In 330, Constantine moved the capital east to the Greek city of Byzantium, which he renamed Constantinople. Constantine took the best Roman artisans, politicians and public figures with him knowing that, with the barbarians closing in, the city of Rome was vulnerable to attack.

For all intents and purposes, Constantinople was the new Rome. In fact, for a time it was even called *Nova Roma*, or New Rome. Rome had become secondary in importance.

A House Divided – Four More Times

When Constantine died in 337, he divided the empire among his sons. When they died, their cousin Julian became the sole emperor, who, turning back the clock, restored paganism in place of Christianity. When he died in 363 (killed in battle), a series of Christian emperors ruled, thus restoring Christianity as the religion of the empire. One of these emperors, Valentinian I, gave control over the Eastern Empire to his brother, Valens, thus dividing the empire into two halves once again.

Around this time, the Huns, a barbarian tribe from Asia, were attacking from the east, forcing the barbarian Gallic and Germanic tribes, including the Visigoths, Vandals, Saxons, Franks, and others, to migrate west. When the Visigoths sought refuge from the Eastern Emperor, Valens, he accommodated them by giving them shelter within Roman territory (on the Roman side of the Danube River). However, he treated them badly and they rebelled, eventually killing Valens in 378 in the Battle of Adrianople. Many consider Valens' accommodation of the Visigoths as the second major mistake that led to Rome's downfall (the first being the division of the empire), as the barbarians were now truly "within the gate."

With Valens dead, the Visogoths rebelling, and other barbarian tribes approaching, Valentinian I (the western emperor) was pretty worked up. He died of a stroke, leaving control of the empire to his 16-year-old son, Gratian. Gratian then appointed his army commander, Theodosius I, as the new eastern emperor, thus dividing the empire again.

Gratian was shortly killed by rebelling troops. His successors faired no better and were eventually defeated by Theodosius in 394, effectively putting the empire under one leader again—for now.

Theodosius ended up signing a peace treaty with the Visigoths, allowing them to settle within Roman territory, armed, and under the direction of their own king (another costly mistake). Eventually, Theodosius's sons, Arcadius and Honorius, inherited the eastern and western empires, respectively (once again dividing the empire). During this period of change, in 395, the Visigoths seized the opportunity to rebel in Constantinople. They eventually settled in Greece and made several unsuccessful invasions of Italy.

The Fall of Rome

In 410 AD, fed up after several years of unsuccessful negotiations with Honorius (the western emperor), the Visigoths sacked Rome. They eventually left and were given a nearby kingdom of their own. However, Honorius and his successors had very little control, and merely became figureheads, while the mostly assimilated Germanic commanders were left to rule the armies.

There were five other major things happening around this time that were also very relevant to the ultimate fall of Rome (which by this time still existed in a weakened state after being sacked):

- As Rome grew over the years, its people became more comfortable and civilized (i.e. fat and happy), which made them somewhat less interested in military concerns and less interested in activism of any kind.

- As taxes increased and the government grew more and more authoritative, people were less and less loyal and trusting of the government. They no longer felt properly represented or that the leaders cared for their well being.

- Famine and plague began to take hold, reducing the population of Rome from over a million people to about 20,000, further disillusioning and weakening the resolve of the people.

- With less resolve and dedication, fewer Roman citizens were willing to become soldiers. As a result, barbarian Germans (and eventually even the Huns) ended up becoming a regular part of the Roman army.

- Gallic and Germanic barbarian tribes had migrated from the north and east, with the Franks and Burgundians moving to France, the Alemanni moving to Germany (the French word for Germany is Allemagne), the Anglo-Saxons (made up of the Angles and the Saxons) moving to Britain (and changing the language from Latin to English), and the Vandals moving to Spain and North Africa. Rome itself became a mélange of peoples.

The result of all this was that the Roman army, made up mostly of foreign soldiers, tended to be less disciplined and certainly less motivated. Napoleon Bonaparte would later share a similar fate, when foreign troops, comprising two-thirds of his army, deserted in droves during his failed Russian campaign in 1812. Likewise, the British fared no better with their Hessian troops during the American Revolutionary War.

Because of this lack of cohesiveness, discipline, and motivation, civil war and rebellion was once again rampant, and the western empire was under continuous attack. Ultimately, Visigoth mutineers ended up ousting what was to be the final emperor of Rome, Romulus Augustus (himself part barbarian). They did not acknowledge his position on the throne, as his father, who had taken it in a military coup, had given it to him. With this ousting, in 476, the western empire (and therefore the Roman Empire) had officially ceased to be—the leader of the revolt, Odoacer, chose not to rule the western empire, but rather to be the King of Italy, ruling from Ravenna, a nearby town. It is somewhat fitting that Rome began with a Romulus and ended with a Romulus.

The city of Rome was left abandoned and in ruins, eventually to be salvaged and run under Papal leadership. The Christian Church grew in power, and it was eventually the Bishops who were able to organize resistance to the barbarians and govern Rome. However, viewing the baths and technological breakthroughs as materialistic excess and an affront to God, these things were abolished. Roman technology would be gone for nearly 1,500 years, as oppression remained through the Dark and Middle Ages. Technology didn't really make a recovery until the 19th century.

Constantinople (now called Istanbul) stood for another thousand years after the fall of Rome as the capital of the great Byzantine Empire. It withstood numerous invasions by Islamic armies in the 7th century, and later by the Crusaders, but was left weakened by years of war. Eventually it was taken over by the Ottoman Turks in 1453.

To some, the Byzantine Empire preserved the last remnants of the Roman Empire, although they eventually reverted to the Greek language and gradually shed Roman customs. To others, the much later "Holy Roman Empire" represented the last ties to ancient Rome; however, it wasn't really Roman (nor, as one author pointed out, was it holy or even much of an empire) but rather was called this because of the kings who chose to be confirmed and crowned "emperor" by the pope. This idea started with Charlemagne, but became officially referred to as The Holy Roman Empire beginning with Otto the Great in 962. It lasted for nearly a thousand years (mostly in Germany) until it was eventually abolished by Napoleon in 1806 when he established the Confederation of the Rhine (a league of German States) after defeating the Austrians at Austerlitz. Two years earlier, Napoleon had planned to be crowned by the pope, but in the end chose to crown himself instead.

CHAPTER ELEVEN

A Matter of Leadership

We have now seen Rome's rise to glory, and its gradual decline and fall. So what did ultimately cause the fall of Rome? Was it bad leadership? The division of the Empire? Plague? Ineffective leaders? Civil war? Growth? Barbarians? Strategic mistakes? In a sense, it was all of the above.

Ineffective leadership certainly played a major role. Rome always had its share of bad emperors (Caligula, Nero, and Commodus being good examples). Fortunately, they didn't last long and there were usually good emperors to correct their errors. In the end, however, good leaders were at a premium and didn't come along frequently enough. In fact, towards the end, great leaders were often killed, as they presented a threat to the emperor. This not only deprived Rome of good leadership, but depleted the army of good generals as well.

Due to a succession of ineffective leaders, who, through their shortsightedness, did not consider the will or the perspective of the people, there was a lack of loyalty or sense of purpose in the citizens of Rome. This was made worse by the poor economy and high taxes. As a result, Rome had to rely on foreign soldiers. No longer were Roman armies inspired or dedicated to a common goal. This was exacerbated by the fact that the Roman Empire itself was divided in half. On top of that, plague was running rampant around this time. When you combine ineffective leadership, divisiveness, plague and lack of dedication, it does not make for a good, cohesive, motivated fighting force, and it's only a matter of time before complete and total breakdown occurs.

One may argue that the growth of Rome made all of this inevitable but it's more likely that a lack of leadership and vision is to blame, especially in the later years. The basic leadership skills of motivation, diplomacy, compassion, and planning for scalability, all such a huge part of the success of prior leaders, was no longer there. Such thinking perhaps could have enabled Rome to remain stable.

So how does this apply to modern-day project management? First, it reiterates our earlier point about ensuring that your team is dedicated to the mission. Find out their concerns and their needs. Make sure their needs are being met, and at the same time, ensure that your needs are met by properly selling and positioning the project.

We can use the loss of people and morale due to plague in ancient Rome as an analogy to the mental and physical health of your team. Don't burn out your people with excessive overtime. Encourage them to keep a balance in their life. Take an interest in their family life and in their health.

Don't allow divisiveness to break up your team. Time and time again, history has shown that divided leadership inevitably leads to potential conflicts and ultimate failure. Likewise, there can only be one project manager ultimately accountable for the success of the project. Certainly, as a project manager, you must confer with your stakeholders but ultimately you are responsible for the outcome of the project. All members of the project team should be sold on the mission, have a clear understanding of the objectives, and should be working in concert with the project manager.

Understand cultural differences and treat people fairly. The two major uprisings by the Visigoths were a result of being treated unfairly. Ultimately, the struggle between the Romans and the barbarians boiled down to a lack of tolerance and understanding for one another's cultural lifestyle. Augustus understood this and was able to maintain peace with the barbarians. If the later emperors were able to identify a win-win solution, they may have been able not only to coexist peacefully, but also to work together to achieve common goals. In addition, conflict management skills would have enabled them to better settle conflicts when they did arise.

Finally, be sure to plan for growth. That is, plan for the ongoing ease of use and maintenance of the product of your project. Consider the entire product lifecycle, not just the project lifecycle. Otherwise, future problems with the product can virtually undo all of the great efforts made during what appeared to be a highly successful project.

To summarize the lessons learned from the fall of Rome:

> Ensure that your team is sold on the project. Consider the
> acronyms MMFI (Make me feel important) and WIIFM
> (What's in it for me?) when considering your team's perspec-
> tive.

> Don't burn out your team with excessive overtime. Encour-
> age a balanced lifestyle. Family and health come even before
> your project.

> Don't confuse your team with multiple messages. There can
> only be one project manager (although the stakeholders'
> interests should always be preserved).

> Make it a point to learn about both cultural awareness and
> conflict management. Avoid making potentially damaging
> mistakes due to ignorance.

> Plan for growth. Consider the product lifecycle when plan-
> ning and designing, not just your project's lifecycle. Make
> your product easy to use and maintain or it can come back to
> haunt you later.

CHAPTER TWELVE

Conclusion and Summary

As leaders, we have a duty to lead responsibly and humanely. Through the lessons of the rise and fall of the Roman Empire, we can perhaps see the impact of our short-term and long-term actions. We can emulate the actions of effective leaders and avoid the shortcomings of bad ones. We began by exploring the underlying principles and strengths of Rome, as well as its weaknesses. We took a high-level tour of the entire Roman history, from monarchy to republic to empire, to its ultimate demise. We examined the causes of its rise, and the reasons for its fall. Along the way, we captured lessons that apply to today's leadership and project management—lessons that can guide us in our everyday actions.

So that you may easily and quickly reference these lessons and apply them in practical use, I will list them below. Let's not forget these valuable lessons:

- Be sure to document lessons learned throughout your project, while things are fresh in your mind. At the end of your project, finalize them in a useful summary format geared toward the intended target audience, not buried in issues lists and change logs. Better yet, keep a database updated with lessons learned by category. *We are only able to learn from the Romans because so much is heavily documented. This learning can be made even easier through concise summarization, packaged with a specific purpose or audience in mind.*

- Make sure to document the business need, tied to a corporate or departmental objective, as part of your project's charter and/or scope statement. This is useful for keeping the team motivated by making the project important, and for providing much needed focus, especially when evaluating future tradeoffs. *Rome did this by tying all of their initiatives to the expansion and betterment of the Roman Empire. Their justification was that the gods wanted them to proliferate civil law throughout the world.*

- To reinforce the importance of your project, give your project a reason for being, and position your project in your team's mind to be better than any alternative (including not doing the project). Make a compelling case by applying business acumen. *The Romans made effective use of positioning by offering security and stability as opposed to tyranny or barbarism.*

- Don't forget the Project Execution phase. What the Romans called "obedience" and we can call "alignment" can be achieved by having clear and agreed-upon goals; assigned work packages; brief, frequent check-ins that include issues, risks, lessons learned, and stakeholder feedback; and good old MBWA (management by walking around). This will allow you to steer the ship into a safe port (as Horace noted that Augustus had done). *Knowing that their leaders always possessed the "big picture," the Romans considered obedience a necessity for success, and discouraged rogue actions.*

- Balance your key roles in life, and never forget the importance of family when setting your priorities. When mingling with your team, be sure to ask about their families to foster this mentality. Improve and renew yourself by making time for reading, exercise, public service, education, and any other hobbies of interest. Encourage your team to do the same. *Family and education were central to the Roman way of life, and to their success.*

- Encourage innovation, but innovate to fill a practical need. Consider small, inexpensive improvements that will delight the customer. Have a formal change management review if the innovations will alter the project's outcomes, duration, or cost. Encourage team participation in innovation. Challenge them to create new best practices that can accomplish the objective faster, less costly or more effectively (or better yet, all three). Finally, don't feel compelled to reinvent the wheel; seek far and wide for existing innovative practices and improve upon them. *All of the Romans' innovations were done for practical reasons, and research into historic best practices was leveraged whenever possible.*

- Know the core competencies needed to accomplish your objectives. Make sure your team is skilled in these competencies. Skill, knowledge, and vision enable innovation. *The Romans recognized engineering as a core competency and fostered it.*

- Always ensure problem-driven solutions; make sure the problem is clearly understood before proposing or implementing solutions. A perfectly implemented but misguided solution serves nobody. *The many Roman inventions and undertakings happened because they needed to solve a problem, not because they were looking for a problem with which to use their technology.*

- To weigh the usefulness of a proposed enhancement, and to ensure problem-driven and client-centric solutions, try developing written customer scenarios that explain how the end user will use the solution. This may expose a lack of need, a better solution, or additional problems to solve. *The Romans used customer scenarios to plan for all possible risks. The same approach can be used to confirm the need for an enhancement, and to ensure that the enhancement solves the problem effectively.*

- Don't reinvent the wheel. It wastes money and overlooks existing solutions. *Many technological innovations of other ancient peoples only survive today because the Romans adopted them.*

- Plan extensively. Make sure your risk management plan allows for disaster, growth, maintainability, and risks to usability. Project plans and risk management plans are dynamic and ever changing, and should be reviewed, updated, and communicated throughout your project. *The Romans planned and analyzed potential risks extensively when preparing to build a city.*

- Make efficient use of repeatable processes through standard templates that are maintained regularly. Make the update of these templates (if necessary) an output of the lessons learned activity, which should be performed at checkpoints throughout the project and at the end of each project. *The Romans did this by having a standard plan, which was used for building all of their cities and towns.*

- Make strategic alliances with suppliers, relevant functional groups, and all stakeholders (including the customer and your team). When marketing your project, be considerate of your stakeholders' perspective and their concerns. Be sure to make strong alliances with your project team by providing the project's reason for being. *The Roman republic was able to expand, despite all odds, by building strategic alliances. Augustus was even able to secure alliances with conquered nations, ensuring years of peace.*

- Lead from behind the scenes. Always look for win-win solutions. Always give your team the credit for successes, and absorb the blame for failures. *Augustus achieved his great success by leading from behind the scenes, while allowing the Senate to get all of the glory. This resulted in both his needs and that of the Senate being met, a true win-win.*

- Never stop learning and always keep an open mind. *Augustus and other successful emperors all were educated, interested in philosophy, dedicated to their craft, and as a result maintained an open mind.*

- Lead with competency and compassion. Be organizationally aware, study effective leadership techniques, and empathize with your stakeholders. *Augustus and other successful emperors demonstrated both competency (through their dedication to learning) and compassion (through their empathy and win-win approach). As a result, they achieved the love and admiration of the people, and unparalleled success.*

- Be goal-oriented and adaptive. Use the right tools for the job at hand. Install organizational administration to bring order out of chaos. Eliminate bureaucracy when faced with extreme situations. Always try to keep bureaucracy to its smallest effective format. *Augustus was able to adapt his approach to the goal at hand. He established discipline to bring order out of chaos; then built allies to ensure a secure and stable environment; created a bureaucracy to effectively manage a large empire; and, finally, he rebuilt the city and the character of the people, laying the foundation to ensure lasting success beyond his years.*

- Especially for large projects, make it a point to study transformational change management. Don't expect buy-in or dedication from people unless you have studied and know how to apply the techniques required for successful transformational change. *Augustus and other successful emperors all knew how to introduce reforms without causing shock or resistance. They understood the cultural and organizational impacts of transformational change, and were able to introduce their reforms with great success.*

- Ensure that your team is sold on the project. Consider the acronyms MMFI (Make me feel important) and WIIFM (What's in it for me?) when considering your team's perspective. *One cause of the Roman Empire's downfall was that the massive expansion of the army, and the increased taxes that went with it, was done without securing buy-in from the people. As a result, people were disillusioned and the army had to resort to using foreign troops.*

- Don't burn out your team with excessive overtime. Encourage a balanced lifestyle. Family and health come even before your project. *In the latter years of the Roman Empire, plague had taken its toll on the population, causing not only health concerns, but morale problems as well. Even in the heights of its glory, Rome had put the health and vitality of its soldiers as a top priority, recognizing that healthy soldiers were alert and powerful soldiers.*

- Don't confuse your team with multiple messages. There can be only one project manager (although the stakeholders' interests should always be preserved). *Toward the end of the Roman Empire (and periodically throughout its history) there were constant power struggles as various army factions favored their own generals as candidates for emperor. Rome was always at its best when there was one undeniable leader who had vision, yet was responsive and adaptive to the needs of the senate and the people.*

- Make it a point to learn about both cultural awareness and conflict management. Avoid making potentially-damaging mistakes due to ignorance. *Cultural awareness and conflict management could have prevented years of recurring wars with the increasingly oppressed and angry barbarian tribes—wars that ultimately had a devastating effect on the empire.*

- Plan for growth. Consider the product's lifecycle when planning and designing, not just your project's lifecycle. Make your product easy to use and maintain or it can come back to haunt you later. *To a degree, the Romans became a victim of their own success. The larger their empire grew, the more difficult it was to manage. Some leaders, such as Augustus, were able to plan for scalability. His reforms made the growing empire manageable, even for 150 years after his death. Others were not as successful managing such a vast empire and adapting to changing needs while considering the long-term impact of their changes. For example, Diocletian chose to split the empire in half, but this turned out to be an ill-fated decision.*

While these lessons aren't new, and indeed are included in most books on leadership and many on project management, it is my sincere hope that the lessons have been reinforced somehow in a unique way; that perhaps some of you will be inspired to explore other episodes in history, with an eye towards applying the lessons to modern day leadership and project management. You never know when some seemingly entirely new idea or approach can come out of an exploration of the past, or when a lesson told time and time again will finally sink in. Lessons sometimes hide in the strangest of places. Read other books in this *Lessons from History* series to learn from other great leaders and situations.

I also hope that you have found this informative and interesting; that perhaps you may look at Roman history, and history in general, with new eyes.

Finally, and most importantly, I hope that the journey has been fun.

Bibliography

Ackerman-Anderson, Linda, and Dean Anderson. *The Change Leader's Roadmap*. San Francisco, CA: Pfeiffer, 2001.

Anderson, Dean, and Linda Ackerman-Anderson, *Beyond Change Management*. San Francisco, CA: Pfeiffer, 2001.

Aurelius, Marcus, *Meditations*. London: Penguin Classics, 2006.

Beckwith, Harry, *Selling the Invisible: A Field Guide to Modern Marketing*. New York: Warner Business Books, 1997.

Caesar, Julius, *The Conquest of Gaul*. New York: Penguin Books, 1983.

Carcopino, Jerome, *Daily Life in Ancient Rome: The People and the City at the Height of the Empire*. New Haven, CT: Yale University Press, 2003.

Charan, Ram, *What the CEO Wants You to Know: How Your Company Really Works*. New York: Crown Business, 2001.

Covey, Stephen R., *The 7 Habits of Highly Effective People*. New York: Free Press, 1990.

Cowell, F.R., *Life in Ancient Rome*. New York: Perigee Trade, 1976.

De Camp, L. Sprague, *The Ancient Engineers*. New York: Ballantine Books, 1995.

DeLuca, Joel R., *Political Savvy: Systematic Approaches to Leadership Behind-the-Scenes*. Berwyn, PA: EBG Publications, 1999.

Dio, Cassius, *The Roman History: The Reign of Augustus*. London: Penguin Classics, 1987.

Everitt, Anthony, *Augustus: The Life of Rome's First Emperor*. New York: Random House, 2007.

Gibbon, Edward, *Decline and Fall of the Roman Empire*. Hertfordshire, UK: Wordsworth Editions, Ltd., 1999.

Goldsworthy, Adrian, *How Rome Fell: Death of a Superpower*. New Haven, CT: Yale University Press, 2009.

Landels, J.G., *Engineering in the Ancient World*. Berkely, CA: University of California Press, 2000.

Macaulay, David, *City – A Story of Roman Planning and Construction*. London: Sandpiper Books, Ltd., 1983.

Manas, Jerry, *Managing the Gray Areas*. Minnetonka, MN: RMC Publications, 2008

Manas, Jerry, *Napoleon on Project Management: Timeless Lessons in Planning, Execution, and Leadership.* Nashville: Nelson Business, 2006.

Moore, Geoffrey, *Crossing the Chasm.* New York: Harper Business, 2002.

Nelson, Eric D., *The Complete Idiot's Guide to The Roman Empire.* New York: Alpha Books, 2001.

Peters, Tom, *The Project 50 (Reinventing Work): Fifty Ways to Transform Every "Task" into a Project That Matters!* New York: Knopf Publishing, 1999.

Polybius, *The Rise of the Roman Empire.* London: Penguin Classics, 1980.

Project Management Institute, *A Guide to the Project Management Body of Knowledge (PMBOK Guide) – 2000 Edition.* Newtown Square, PA: Project Management Institute, 2000.

Scarre, Chris, *The Penguin Historical Atlas of Ancient Rome.* New York: Penguin, 1995.

Shelton, Jo-Ann, *As the Romans Did: A Sourcebook in Roman Social History.* New York: Oxford University Press (USA), 1998.

Suetonius, *The Twelve Caesars.* London: Penguin Classics, 2007.

Tacitus, *The Annals of Imperial Rome.* London: Penguin Classics, 1956.

Tingay, Graham, and Anthony Marks, *The Usborne Illustrated World History: The Romans.* Tulsa, OK: E.D.C. Publishing, 1990.

Websites

PBS Empires: The Roman Empire. <http://www.pbs.org/empires/romans/>.

Roman History, Coins, and Technology Back Pages. <http://www.jaysromanhistory.com/>.

The Illustrated History of the Roman Empire. <http://www.roman-empire.net/>.

About the Author

Jerry Manas is the author of *Managing the Gray Areas* (RMC Publications, January 2008) and the international bestseller *Napoleon on Project Management* (Nelson Business, April 2006), and co-author of *42 Rules for Creating WE* (Superstar Press, September 2009). His work, which is at the crossroads of project management and organizational development, has been cited by management guru Tom Peters and highlighted in a variety of publications, including *Leadership Excellence*, *The National Post*, *The Globe and Mail*, *The Chicago Sun Times*, and *The Houston Chronicle*. He has written numerous articles and appeared on radio programs nationwide with the release of his first book, which Kirkus Reviews called, "The ultimate case study in effective project management."

Through his consulting company, The Marengo Group, Jerry focuses on the human side of project management, helping organizations and teams establish the identity, culture, and communication necessary for breakthrough performance. This results in:

- Highly motivated and better aligned people;
- Faster achievement of core objectives; and
- More productive use of enabling technology.

Centering his work on the core principles of simplicity, engagement, and trust (SET™), Jerry is passionate about helping leaders create energized teams that are aligned and focused toward shared goals.

Jerry is co-founder of the popular leadership and project management blog site, PMThink!, and a founding member of The Creating We Institute, an international group of critical thinkers dedicated to harvesting new forms of engagement and innovation in the workforce. In addition to his extensive consulting career, he has managed numerous large-scale, global programs spanning Europe, Asia/Pacific, Latin America, and North America.

Jerry is an active volunteer with the Project Management Institute (PMI), and was recently named to PMI's New Media Council as an influential voice in the online project management community. He has contributed to several of PMI's international standards, including their Organizational Project Management Maturity Model (OPM3) and their standards for Program and Portfolio Management, where he served on the core leadership team.

With an endless curiosity, a passion for research, and a

deep interest in multiple disciplines, including history, science, philosophy, and more, he often writes on lessons learned from unexpected places and frequently speaks on the topic to business leaders and university students.

Contact Jerry at: jmanas@marengogroup.com or on Twitter @jmanas

LESSONS FROM
HISTORY

About the Series

This series is for primarily business and IT professionals looking for inspiration for their projects. Specifically, business managers responsible for solving business problems, or Project Managers (PMs) responsible for delivering business solutions through IT projects.

This series uses relevant historical case studies to examine how historical projects and emerging technologies of the past solved complex problems. It then draws comparisons to challenges encountered in today's IT projects.

This series benefits the reader in several ways:

- It outlines the stages involved in delivering a complex IT project providing a step-by-step guide to the project deliverables.

- It vividly describes the crucial lessons from historical projects and complements these with some of today's best practices.

- It makes the whole learning experience more memorable.

The series should inspire the reader as these historical projects were achieved with a lesser (inferior) technology.

Website: **http://www.lessons-from-history.com/**

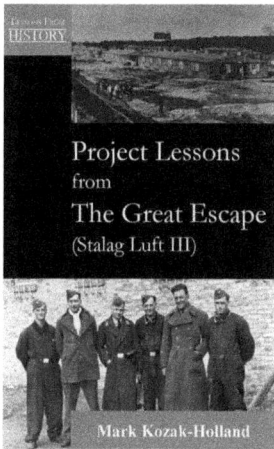

Project Lessons from The Great Escape (Stalag Luft III)

While you might think your project plan is perfect, would you bet your life on it?

In World War II, a group of 220 captured airmen did just that — they staked the lives of everyone in the camp on the success of a project to secretly build a series of tunnels out of a prison camp their captors thought was escape proof.

The prisoners formally structured their work as a project, using the project organization techniques of the day. This book analyzes their efforts using modern project management methods and the nine knowledge areas of the *Guide to the Project Management Body of Knowledge* (PMBoK).

Learn from the successes and mistakes of a project where people really put their lives on the line.

ISBN: 1-895186-80-3   (paperback)
Also available in ebook formats.

http://www.mmpubs.com/escape

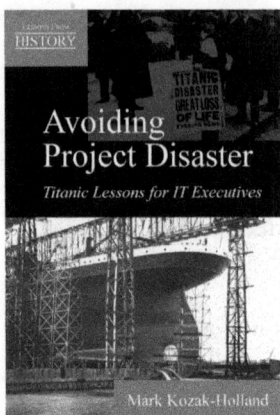

Avoiding Project Disaster: Titanic Lessons for IT Executives

Imagine you are in one of *Titanic's* lifeboats. As you look back at the wreckage, you wonder what could have happened. What were the causes? How could things have gone so badly wrong?

Titanic's maiden voyage was a disaster waiting to happen as a result of the compromises made in the project that constructed the ship. This book explores how modern executives can take lessons from a nuts-and-bolts construction project like *Titanic* and use those lessons to ensure the right approach to developing online business solutions.

Avoiding Project Disaster is about delivering IT projects in a world where being on time and on budget is not enough. You also need to be up and running around the clock for your customers and partners. This book will help you successfully maneuver through the ice floes of IT management in an industry with a notoriously high project failure rate.

ISBN: 1-895186-73-0   (paperback)
Also available in ebook formats.

http://www.mmpubs.com/disaster

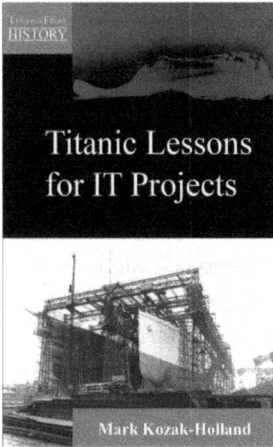

Titanic Lessons for IT Projects

Titanic Lessons for IT Projects analyzes the project that designed, built, and launched the ship, showing how compromises made during early project stages led to serious flaws in this supposedly "perfect ship." In addition, the book explains how major mistakes during the early days of the ship's operations led to the disaster. All of these disasterous compromises and mistakes were fully avoidable.

Entertaining and full of intriguing historical details, this companion book to *Avoiding Project Disaster: Titanic Lessons for IT Executives* helps project managers and IT executives see the impact of decisions similar to the ones that they make every day. An easy read full of illustrations and photos to help explain the story and to help drive home some simple lessons.

ISBN: 1-895186-26-9   (paperback)
Also available in ebook formats.

http://www.mmpubs.com/titanic

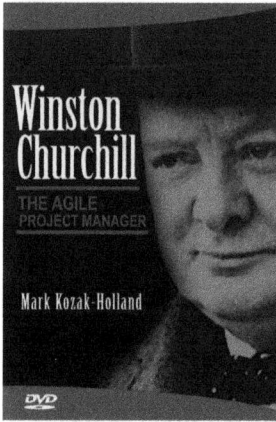

Winston Churchill, The Agile Project Manager

In May 1940, the United Kingdom (UK) was facing a dire situation, an imminent invasion. As the evacuation of Dunkirk unfolded, the scale of the disaster became apparent. The army abandoned 90% of its equipment, the RAF fighter losses were deplorable, and over 200 ships were lost.

Winston Churchill, one of the greatest leaders of the 20th century, was swept into power. With depleted forces and no organized defense, the situation required a near miracle. Churchill had to mobilize quickly and act with agility to assemble a defense. He had to make the right investment choices, pour resources in, and deliver a complete project in time to save his country. This audio looks at Churchill as an agile Project Manger, turning a disastrous situation into an unexpected victory.

ISBN: 1-895186-50-1 (audio CD)
ISBN: 1-897326-38-6 (DVD)

http://www.PM-Audiobooks.com

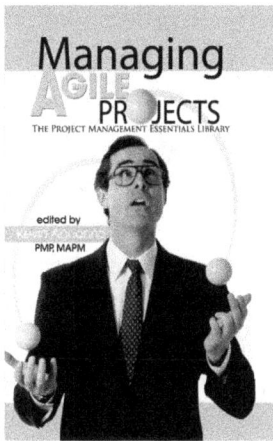

Managing Agile Projects

Are you being asked to manage a project with unclear requirements, high levels of change, or a team using Extreme Programming or other Agile Methods?

If you are a project manager or team leader who is interested in learning the secrets of successfully controlling and delivering agile projects, then this is the book for you.

From learning how agile projects are different from traditional projects, to detailed guidance on a number of agile management techniques and how to introduce them onto your own projects, this book has the insider secrets from some of the industry experts – the visionaries who developed the agile methodologies in the first place.

ISBN: 1-895186-11-0   (paperback)
ISBN: 1-895186-12-9   (PDF ebook)

http://www.agilesecrets.com

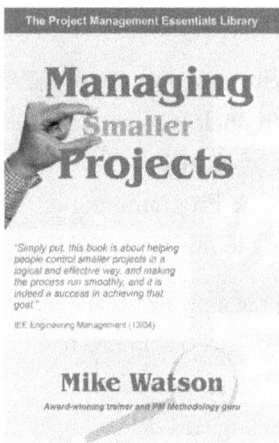

Managing Smaller Projects: A Practical Approach

So called "small projects" can have potentially alarming consequences if they go wrong, but their control is often left to chance. The solution is to adapt tried and tested project management techniques.

This book provides a low overhead, highly practical way of looking after small projects. It covers all the essential skills: from project start-up, to managing risk, quality and change, through to controlling the project with a simple control system. It cuts through the jargon of project management and provides a framework that is as useful to those lacking formal training, as it is to those who are skilled project managers and want to control smaller projects without the burden of bureaucracy.

Read this best-selling book from the U.K., now making its North American debut. *IEE Engineering Management* praises the book, noting that "Simply put, this book is about helping people control smaller projects in a logical and effective way, and making the process run smoothly, and is indeed a success in achieving that goal."

Available in print format.

http://www.mmpubs.com/msp

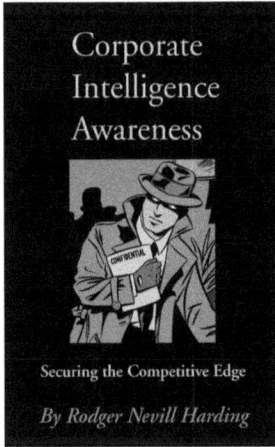

Corporate
Intelligence
Awareness

Securing the Competitive Edge

By Rodger Nevill Harding

Corporate Intelligence Awareness: Securing the Competitive Edge

In this compelling new book by a former diplomat, you will learn the secrets (step by step) to developing an intelligence strategy by effective information gathering and analyzing, and then to delivering credible intelligence to senior management. Along the way, you will learn how to better read people and organizations and get them to open up and share information with you—all the while behaving in an ethical, legal manner. Understanding how intelligence is gathered and processed will keep you ahead of the game, protect your secrets, and secure your competitive edge!

ISBN: 1-895186-42-0   (hardcover)
ISBN: 1-895186-43-9   (PDF ebook)

Also available in other ebook formats.

http://www.mmpubs.com/cia

Want to Get Ahead in Your Career?

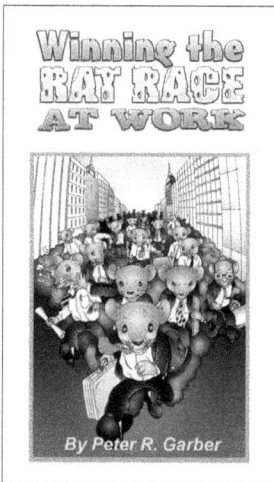
By Peter R. Garber

Do you find yourself challenged by office politics, bad things happening to good careers, dealing with the "big cheeses" at work, the need for effective networking skills, and keeping good working relationships with coworkers and bosses? *Winning the Rat Race at Work* is a unique book that provides you with case studies, interactive exercises, self-assessments, strategies, evaluations, and models for overcoming these workplace challenges. The book illustrates the stages of a career and the career choices that determine your future, empowering you to make positive changes.

Written by Peter R. Garber, the author of *100 Ways to Get on the Wrong Side of Your Boss*, this book is a must read for anyone interested in getting ahead in his or her career. You will want to keep a copy in your top desk drawer for ready reference whenever you find yourself in a challenging predicament at work.

ISBN: 1-895186-68-4   (paperback)
Also available in ebook formats.

http://www.mmpubs.com/rats

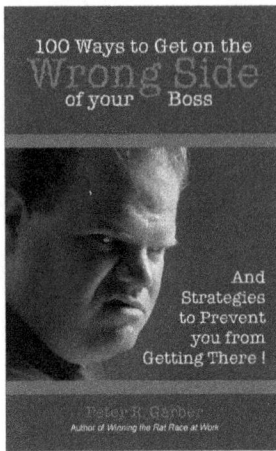

Need More Help with the Politics at Work?

100 Ways To Get On The Wrong Side Of Your Boss (And Strategies to Prevent You from Getting There!) was written for anyone who has ever been frustrated by his or her working relationship with the boss— and who hasn't ever felt this way! Bosses play a critically important role in your career success and getting on the wrong side of this important individual in your working life is not a good thing.

Each of these 100 Ways is designed to illustrate a particular problem that you may encounter when dealing with your boss and then an effective strategy to prevent this problem from reoccurring. You will learn how to deal more effectively with your boss in this fun and practical book filled with invaluable advice that can be utilized every day at work.

Written by Peter R. Garber, the author of *Winning the Rat Race at Work*, this book is a must read for anyone inter-ested in getting ahead. You will want to keep a copy in your top desk drawer for ready reference whenever you find yourself in a challenging predicament at work.

ISBN: 1-895186-98-6   (paperback)
Also available in ebook formats.

http://www.InTroubleAtWork.com

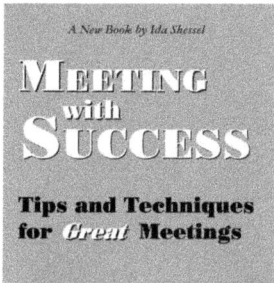

www.ingramcontent.com/pod-product-compliance
Lightning Source LLC
Chambersburg PA
CBHW070817100426
42742CB00012B/2388